Tours

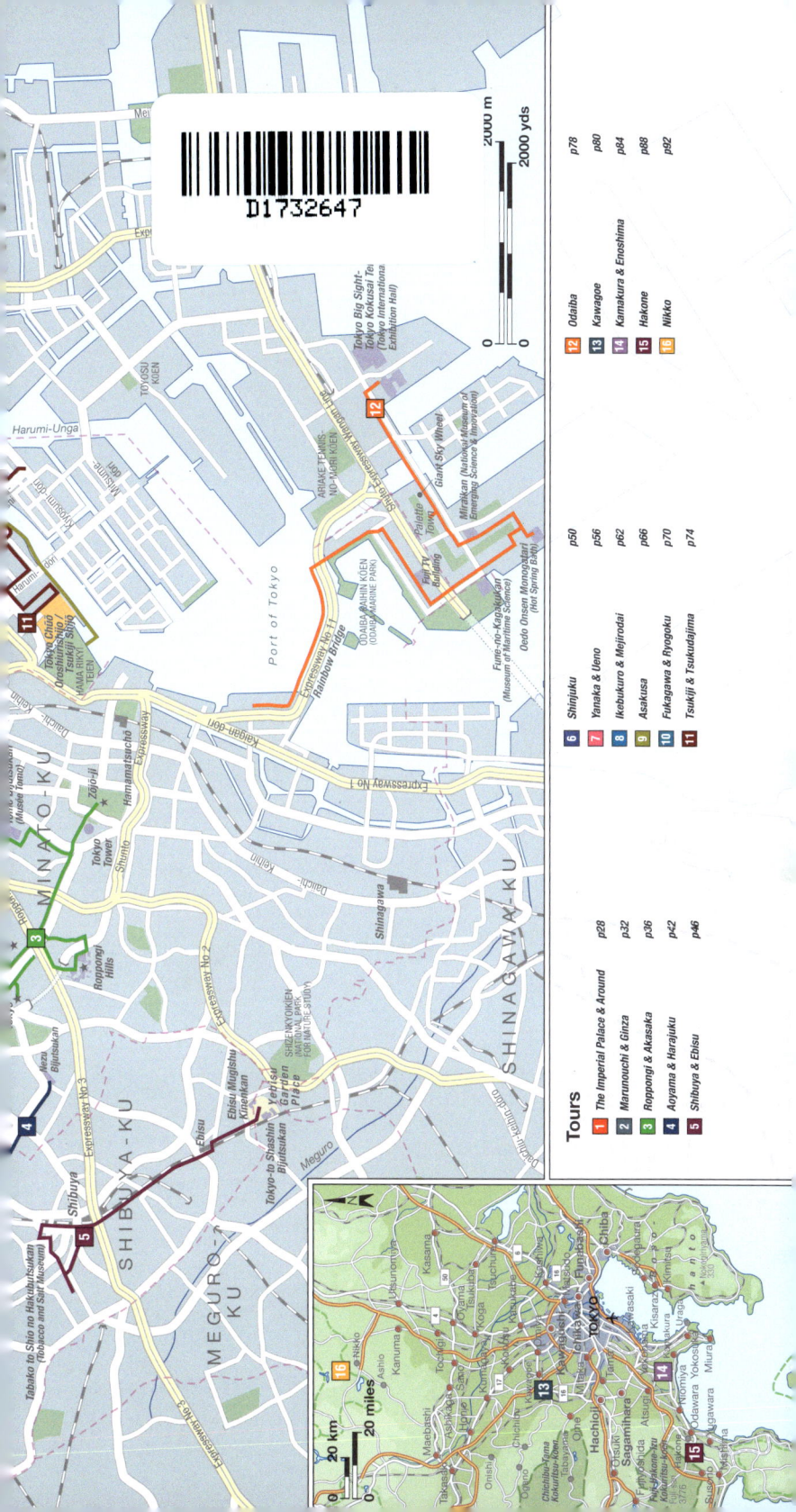

1	The Imperial Palace & Around	p28
2	Marunouchi & Ginza	p32
3	Roppongi & Akasaka	p36
4	Aoyama & Harajuku	p42
5	Shibuya & Ebisu	p46
6	Shinjuku	p50
7	Yanaka & Ueno	p56
8	Ikebukuro & Mejirodai	p62
9	Asakusa	p66
10	Fukagawa & Ryogoku	p70
11	Tsukiji & Tsukudajima	p74
12	Odaiba	p78
13	Kawagoe	p80
14	Kamakura & Enoshima	p84
15	Hakone	p88
16	Nikko	p92

INSIGHT GUIDES
TOKYO
Step by Step

APA PUBLICATIONS
Part of the Langenscheidt Publishing Group

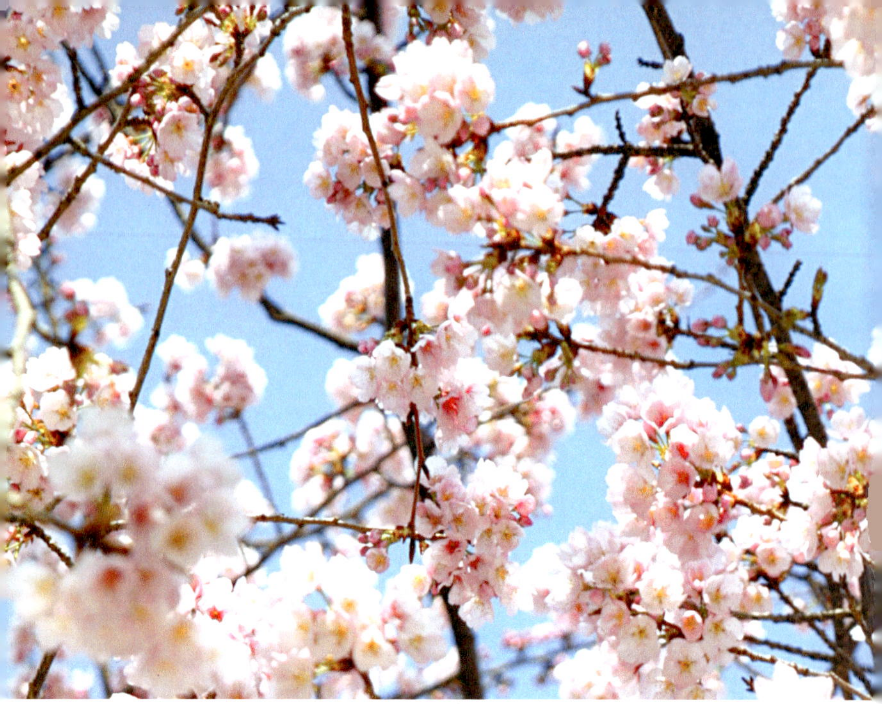

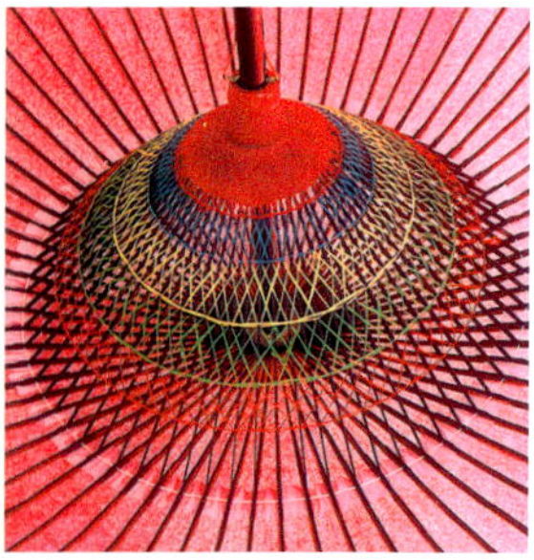

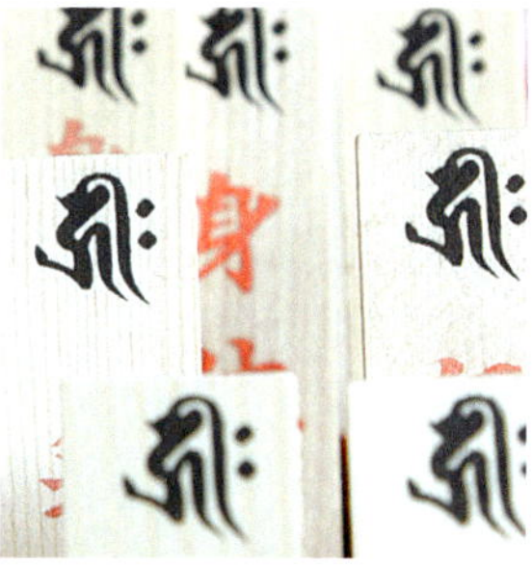

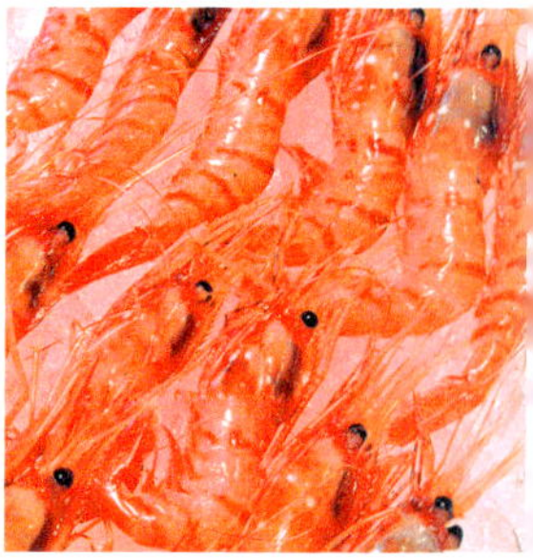

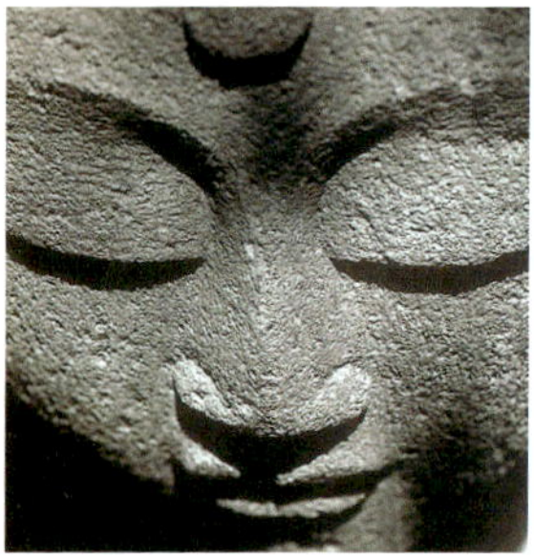

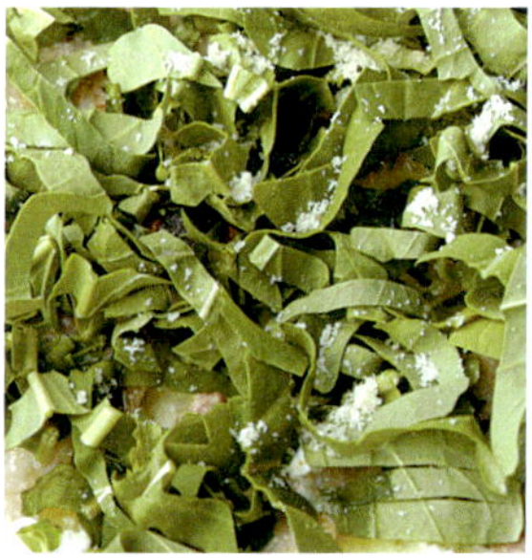

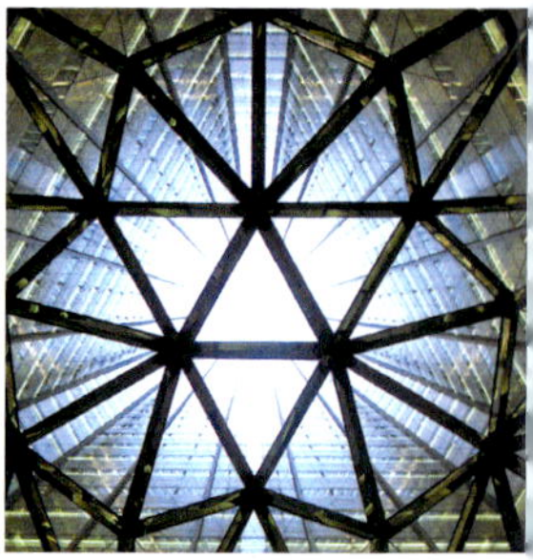

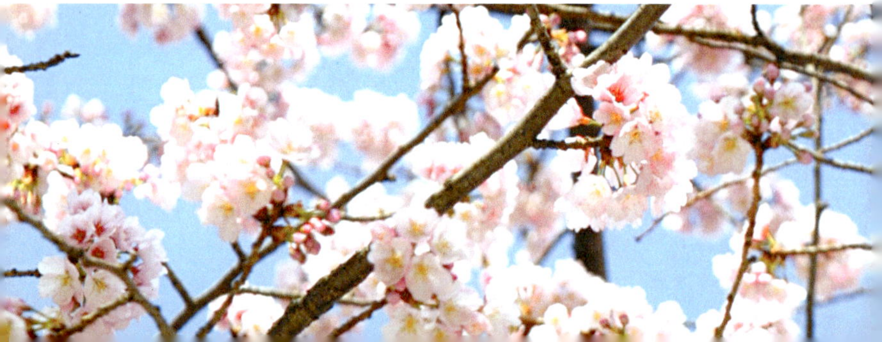

CONTENTS

Introduction
About this Book 4
Recommended Tours 6

Overview
City Introduction 10
Food & Drink 14
Shopping 18
Sports & Entertainment 20
History: Key Dates 24

Walks & Tours
1. The Imperial Palace & Around 28
2. Marunouchi & Ginza 32
3. Roppongi & Akasaka 36
4. Aoyama & Harajuku 42
5. Shibuya & Ebisu 46
6. Shinjuku 50
7. Yanaka & Ueno 56
8. Ikebukuro & Mejirodai 62
9. Asakusa 66
10. Fukagawa & Ryogoku 70
11. Tsukiji & Tsukudajima 74
12. Odaiba 78
13. Kawagoe 80
14. Kamakura & Enoshima 84
15. Hakone 88
16. Nikko 92

Directory
A–Z of Practical Information 98
Accommodation 108
Restaurants 114
Nightlife 120

Credits & Index
Picture Credits 124
Index 126

ABOUT THIS BOOK

This *Step by Step Guide* has been produced by the editors of Insight Guides, whose books have set the standard for visual travel guides since 1970. With top-quality photography and authoritative recommendations, this guidebook brings you the very best of Tokyo in a series of 16 tailor-made tours.

WALKS AND TOURS

The tours in the book provide something to suit all budgets, tastes and trip lengths. As well as covering Tokyo's many classic attractions, the routes track lesser-known sights and up-and-coming areas; there are also excursions for those who want to extend their visit outside the city. The tours embrace a range of interests, so whether you are an art fan, a gourmet, a history buff or have kids to entertain, you will find an option to suit.

We recommend that you read the whole of a tour before setting out. This should help you to familiarise yourself with the route and enable you to plan where to stop for refreshments – options for this are shown in the 'Food and Drink' boxes, recognisable by the knife-and-fork sign.

For our pick of the walks by theme, consult Recommended Tours For… *(see pp.6–7).*

OVERVIEW

The tours are set in context by this introductory section, giving an overview of the city to set the scene, plus background information on food and drink, shopping, sports and entertainment. A succinct history timeline highlights the key events that have shaped Tokyo over the centuries.

DIRECTORY

Also supporting the tours is a Directory chapter, comprising a clearly organised A–Z of practical information, our pick of where to stay while you are in the city and select restaurant listings; these eateries complement the more low-key cafés and restaurants that feature within the tours and are intended to offer a wider choice for evening dining. Also included here are some nightlife listings.

Above: Namco Namjatown, Ikebukuro; Hama Rikyu Garden; the National Sumo Stadium is in riverside Ryogoku; Shinkansen, the bullet train; Gokoku-ji.

The Authors

Stephen Mansfield is a British-born writer and photographer who has spent many years living in Japan. He has written extensively on themes connected to Asia and Japan, in publications as diverse as *The Geographical*, *Newsweek* and the *South China Morning Post*.

Travel writer and photographer Simon Richmond (www.simonrichmond.com) developed an instant crush on Tokyo when he arrived in the early 1990s to work for two and a half years as an editor at a financial newspaper and city listings magazine. He has returned every year or so for over a decade, exploring it mainly on foot, getting lost in its fascinating maze of streets and making many happy discoveries on the way, usually of a culinary variety.

Margin Tips
Shopping tips, historical facts, handy hints and information on activities help visitors to make the most of their time in Tokyo.

Feature Boxes
Notable topics are highlighted in these special boxes.

Key Facts Box
This box gives details of the distance covered on the tour, plus an estimate of how long it should take. It also states where the route starts and finishes, and gives key travel information such as which days are best to do the route or handy transport tips.

Footers
Look here for the tour name, a map reference and the main attraction on the double-page.

Food and Drink
Recommendations of where to stop for refreshment are given in these boxes. The numbers prior to each restaurant/café name link to references in the main text. Restaurants in the Food and Drink boxes are plotted on the maps.

The ¥ signs at the end of each entry reflect the approximate cost of a three-course meal for one, excluding beverages. These should be seen as a guide only. Price ranges, also quoted on the inside back flap for easy reference, are:

¥¥¥¥ over ¥5,000
¥¥¥ ¥3,000–5,000
¥¥ ¥1,000–3,000
¥ below ¥1,000

Route Map
Detailed cartography shows the tour clearly plotted with numbered dots. For more detailed mapping, see the pull-out map slotted inside the back cover.

ABOUT THIS BOOK 5

ARCHITECTURE

Omotesando (walk 4) is a veritable catwalk of modern architecture, but Odaiba (walk 12), Shinjuku (walk 6), Marunouchi (walk 2) and Roppongi (walk 3) also sport striking buildings.

RECOMMENDED TOURS FOR...

SCIENCE & TECHNOLOGY

Check out the Miraikan in Odaiba (walk 12), Tokyo's best science museum, while in Shinjuku (walk 6) there's also the fascinating NTT Intercommunication Centre and in Shibuya a museum devoted to electricity (walk 5).

CHILDREN

Youngsters will love riding the monorail and giant Ferris wheel in Odaiba (walk 12) and the cable car and fantasy galleons at Hakone (tour 15). For toys, there's also Kiddyland in Harajuku (walk 4).

ESCAPING THE CROWDS

Meiji-jingu's grounds (walk 4) can be a haven of peace, but to escape the crowds fully, head to the Kiyosumi Garden (walk 10) or the hills surrounding Kamakura (tour 14) or Nikko (tour 16).

FOOD & DRINK

Tsukiji Fish Market (walk 11) is a must, as is Isetan's fantastic food hall (walk 6). Journey out to Kawagoe (tour 13) to enjoy traditional dishes in an old Edo setting.

ART ENTHUSIASTS

Bounce around Roppongi's Art Triangle (walk 3), then dip into Harajuku's anarchic Design Festa (walk 4) or the contemporary galleries of Fukagawa (walk 10).

PARKS & GARDENS

Chinzan-so (walk 8) is a magnificent traditional garden. The Imperial Palace grounds and Hibiya Park (walk 1) are also worth seeing, as is Shinjuku National Garden (walk 6), which offers three styles of garden in one.

HISTORICAL TOKYO

Walk a circuit of the Imperial Palace (walk 1), learn about the city's history at the Edo-Tokyo Museum (walk 10) and get a grand overview at Tokyo National Museum (walk 7).

SHOPPING

Fashionistas should set their compasses for Ginza (walk 2), Aoyama and Harajuku (walk 4), and Shibuya (walk 5). For local crafts, Asakusa (walk 9) and Yanaka (walk 7) have rich pickings.

WATERSIDE VIEWS

Stroll beside the Sumida River (walk 10) or cruise along it from Asakusa (walk 9) into Tokyo Bay, which you can also get a great view of from the Rainbow Bridge (walk 12).

沢の鶴
芳醇無比
沢の鶴
芳醇無比
登録商標
清酒
鳳陽
宮城の美酒
登録商標
芳醇清酒

富樫左衛門

芳醇無比
日本醇良清酒
登録
商標
酒
王

OVERVIEW

An overview of Tokyo's geography, customs and culture, plus illuminating background information on food and drink, shopping, sports, entertainment and history.

CITY INTRODUCTION	10
FOOD & DRINK	14
SHOPPING	18
SPORTS & ENTERTAINMENT	20
HISTORY: KEY DATES	24

CITY INTRODUCTION

A concrete, steel and neon sprawl stretching seemingly to infinity, the world's largest megalopolis is not the most obvious place to discover on foot. However, walking through Tokyo is the best way to experience the city's fascinating history, electrifying hyperactivity and pockets of serenity.

At first glance, Tokyo comes across as a haphazard urban experiment in danger of spinning out of control. Closer examination reveals an organically evolved spoke-and-ring system with the Imperial Palace at its centre. The city's central 23 wards *(ku)* are home to 12.8 million people and interact like a huddle of micro-cities, each wired up by a complex but highly efficient system of underground and overground railway tracks.

The city's full metropolitan area covers 2,168 sq km (837 sq miles), including 27 smaller cities, 14 towns and 27,000 islands, and has a population of 35.2 million. From neighbouring prefectures, millions more head into the centre every day to work and play – you will seldom escape the crowds, but that doesn't mean that you won't also be able to find havens of peace and tranquillity.

Below: the cherry-blossom season is in early April.

TRADITION & CULTURE

For all its modernity, Tokyo is a city imbued with the past, where the traditions and culture of Edo (Tokyo's pre-mid-19th-century name) are cherished. Between its Postmodernist architecture and elevated expressways lie hundreds of temples, shrines and Buddhist statues. You can find the city's premier Buddhist temple in Asakusa *(see p.67)*, the top Shinto shrine Meiji-jingu in Harajuku *(see p.45)* and the controversial shrine Yasukuni-jinja *(see p.28)* near the spacious grounds of the Imperial Palace, the peaceful eye at the centre of Tokyo's storm.

Even though it lacks the greenery of other major cities, Tokyo has a number of formal gardens – often remnants of old Edo estates – where you can enjoy quiet contemplation and the passing of the seasons with beautiful flower displays. There's also a wide range of craft shops and schools for the traditional arts that help maintain skills honed over centuries. Look carefully and you will begin to see how this illustrious heritage is reflected in the designs and meticulous attention to detail of Tokyo's skyscrapers, transport system, modern-art galleries and even hi-tech electronics.

GETTING AROUND

Even though the city is spread out, getting around is easily done using the subway and the Japan Railways (JR) Yamanote line. The latter's egg-shaped track takes roughly an hour to complete a full loop around the inner city. Most of Tokyo's top sights, as well as major hotels and nightspots, are located at or near one of its stops. Partly shadowing the Yamanote beneath ground but describing a wider circle that takes in areas east of the Sumida River is the Oedo subway line.

Places outside the Yamanote line tend to form part of Shitamachi ('Low City'), such as Asakusa and Ryogoku *(see p.66 and p.72)*, or represent the modern face of the city, such as the futuristic landfill island of Odaiba *(see p.78)*.

LIFE IN TOKYO

Visitors to Tokyo are likely to receive the impression of a well-fed, stylishly dressed and orderly society. Despite recent recessions, Tokyo's standard of living remains high – to the outside eye it appears hardly reduced from the giddy days of the late 1980s. Nevertheless, one segment of the population that has grown in recent years is the homeless, some vagrants, many of them elderly or victims of economic hard times. Remarkably, their 'homes' – cardboard boxes and blue tarpaulin tents in the city's major parks – are kept neat and tidy.

Islands of Garbage

Tokyo has come up with an ingenious solution to deal with the mountains of garbage generated by its millions of citizens. Tokyo Bay is home to the euphemistically named Dream Island (Yume no Shima), which is composed entirely of rubbish. Started in the 1960s, Yume no Shima has since been covered by topsoil and now hosts a sports park, tropical greenhouse and waste facility. The building of further 'Dream Islands' in Tokyo Bay continues.

In the past few decades the city's garbage-disposal rules have become increasingly stringent. Visitors can do their part by separating their rubbish into burnables (kitchen waste, cloth and paper), non-burnables (plastics, metals and ceramics) and recyclables (PET bottles, newspapers, cardboard and batteries). You will find dump-bins for each kind of waste in most public facilities, including railway and subway stations.

Above from far left: neon lights of the world's largest megalopolis; Kaminarimon – the entrance to Senso-ji, also known as the Asakusa Kannon Temple; young Tokyoites; prayer cards at Gokoku-ji.

Above from left: rainy reflections in Shinjuku; capsule hotels are a famous answer to the city's lack of space; Mount Fuji; Sanja Matsuri, a notable festival in May.

DIVERSITY & COURTESY

Although Japan as a whole remains strikingly mono-cultural, Tokyo is becoming an increasingly diverse and international metropolis. Young people are attracted to the city's less restricted lifestyles. Foreign students come to study, expats to fulfil contracts. Travellers make money (by teaching English or working in bars and clubs) and have fun. Today, the city has 350,000 resident foreigners, with large numbers of Koreans, Chinese, Japanese-Brazilians, Filipinos and some Westerners settling here.

Few cities in the world can be so populous and yet so cordial in welcoming guests. Tokyoites might not throw their homes open to you (many live in cramped shoebox apartments), but they will often go out of their way to treat you with courtesy and be helpful, even when their English-language skills fail them. Take the trouble to learn a little Japanese before arriving and you will encounter an even warmer welcome. For some pointers on etiquette, *see p.100*.

CLIMATE

Apart from the regular four distinct seasons, Tokyo also has a humid rainy season, which runs from June through to July. Spring, especially early April when the cherry blossoms are out, is delightful. Summers bring humid, subtropical heat well into September, when strong winds and typhoons are common. Autumn has a high sunshine count. Days are often blessed with clear, blue skies, the evenings pleasantly cool and the foliage superb. Winters are relatively mild and snow-free.

FABULOUS FESTIVALS

Matsuri (festivals) have always been integral to the life of Tokyo, and hardly a week goes by without a celebration. Timing your visit to attend one is highly recommended, since not only can they be colourful affairs but they are also a chance to see the usually decorous Japanese letting their hair and inhibitions down. Top events include May's Sanja Matsuri *(see p.69)*, August's Fukagawa Matsuri *(see p.69)* and October's Kawagoe Matsuri *(see p.82)*. Linked to the seasons and to religious beliefs, *matsuri* not only give thanks, petition the gods for favours and promote community solidarity; they also celebrate the sheer joy of life.

There are also local festivals, especially in the summer, that often seem more like community street parties, with plenty of food and drink and spectacular historical recreations, such as the interment of the first Tokugawa shogun, held in Nikko *(see p.92)* bi-annually on 18 May and 17 October.

SHAKY GROUND

One need only look to the horizon to see Mount Fuji, an active volcano, to be reminded of the precarious state in which Tokyoites have always gone about their lives. Japan lies above the confluence of four tectonic plates: the Eurasian, North American, Philippine and Pacific. Home to 20 percent of the world's most powerful earthquakes, the country's most recent massive jolt was the 1995 Great Hanshin Earthquake that took over 5,000 lives. The Great Kanto Earthquake of 1923 flattened large parts of Tokyo and claimed over 58,000 lives, while a July 2007 earthquake that shook Japan's largest nuclear power plant only a few hundred kilometres from Tokyo was a recent reminder of the city's vulnerability to a major tremor.

Even with improved building regulations and techniques, it is estimated by the Japanese government that a quake measuring 7.3 on the Richter scale hitting the city at evening rush hour would kill 13,000 inhabitants and cause $US1 trillion worth of damage. For tips on what to do in the event of a tremor, *see p.99*.

ESCAPING THE CITY

For all its human energy and consumer glitz, there comes a time when even the most hardened urbanites wish to shake off Tokyo's concrete shell. Thanks to an efficient rail system, escape is easily at hand. Depending on one's fancy, choose from old-world Kawagoe *(see p.80)*, Zen-like Kamakura *(see p.84)*, the beautiful lakeside national parkland of Hakone *(see p.88)* or temple-crammed Nikko *(see p.92)*. All of these – not to mention broad Pacific beaches and the soaring peak of Mount Fuji – are within two hours' reach of downtown.

It should be remembered, however, that fully leaving the city behind can be a challenging prospect – especially at the weekend, when it seems as if all of Tokyo is also heading for the great outdoors.

National Holidays
Three times a year almost all of Japan is on holiday. Avoid trips during the New Year (roughly 25 Dec– 4 Jan), Golden Week (29 Apr–5 May) and Obon (7–10 days centring on 15 Aug).

Bus & Cycle Tours

Tired of walking? Organised half- and full-day bus tours of the city and surroundings with English guides and often hotel pick-ups can be arranged via Hato Bus (tel: 3435 6081; www.hatobus.com), Japan Gray Line (tel: 3595 5939; www.jgl.co.jp/inbound) and Sunrise Tours (tel: 5796 5454; www.jtb-sunrisetours.jp).

Tokyo Great Cycling Tour (tel: 4590 2995; www.tokyo cycling.jp) offers two six-hour guided cycle-tour options, each at ¥10,000. Saturday's itinerary heads out to Tokyo Bay and Odaiba, while Sunday's Sumo Route takes you across to Ryogoku.

For something a little different, try Experience Japan (tel: 5328 4030; http://hisexperience.jp). This company offers tours based around a wide range of cultural experiences, including how to make sushi, practise samurai swordsmanship and do *taiko* drumming.

FOOD & DRINK

Tokyo is not known as the Big Sushi for nothing – its variety and quality of food and drink is unrivalled. Here you will sample the very best, from sake and exquisite kaiseki ryori morsels to delicious coffee and croissants.

Japanese cuisine is a sensation for the eyes and the taste buds. Seasoning is minimal, and every chef takes freshness very seriously. Tokyo claims many Japanese dishes as its own, but its cuisine also reflects that of the entire country. Tokyo's gastronomic offerings also encompass other Asian cuisines, as well as those of Europe, Africa and the Americas.

WHERE TO EAT

Neighbourhood Japanese diners are not usually fancy, but the prices are low. Noodle shops are found everywhere, ranging from venerable establishments to cheap stand-and-slurp counters. Conveyor-belt sushi is good value, while *okonomiyaki* (a kind of savoury pancake) make for fun dining. Department stores and shopping malls always offer a wide range of restaurants, usually located on a single floor.

In the evening, *izakaya* (restaurant-pubs) serve reasonably priced local food and alcohol. They typically identify themselves with a string of red lanterns hanging over the door. *Izakaya* do not serve full-course meals, and there is no pressure to eat quickly. Order beer, sake or *sochu* (a vodka-like spirit) and sample a few dishes such as *sashimi*, grilled fish, *yakitori* or tofu. End your meal with rice or noodles.

What Will it Cost?

Eating out in Tokyo is not as expensive as one might expect, especially the lunch set menus for under ¥1,500. For dinner expect to pay about ¥3,000–5,000 per head. Top places can go up to ¥10,000 per person or more.

JAPANESE CUISINE

Japanese cooking focuses on accentuating the inherent flavours rather than enhancing them with sauces. Meals are based on fish, vegetables, seaweed and tofu. Eggs, meat and poultry are used in limited quantities, while dairy foods play no part in the traditional diet. Portions are small and served in bite-sized morsels, with ingredients reflecting the seasons. Presentation is equally important, as the Japanese believe you also eat with your eyes. Plates, bowls and utensils are made of ceramic, glass, stone, wood or lacquer. Like the ingredients, they are changed to fit the season and to match the food they are showcasing.

Food Halls

If you are at a loss for what to eat, the lavish food halls in department store basements known as *depachika* can satisfy any taste. The best can be found in smart department stores like Isetan *(see p.54)* and Mitsukoshi *(see p.35)*.

Sushi & Sashimi

The Japanese love to eat seafood as close as possible to its natural state – either as *sashimi*, slices of raw fish served with a dip of soy sauce and *wasabi* (horseradish), or as sushi, on vinegared rice. The best-known sushi is the Tokyo style known as *nigiri-sushi*. Some of the best *sushiya* (sushi shops) are found near the central fish market in Tsukiji *(see p.74)*.

Although guaranteed to be memorable, dining at a top sushi restaurant can be a dauntingly expensive experience. The cheaper alternative is a *kaiten-zushi* shop, where small dishes of sushi pass by on a conveyor belt, sometimes for as little as ¥100 per plate.

Hotpots

One of the pleasures of visiting Japan in winter is the chance to sample a variety of hearty hotpots. Known as *nabe-ryori* (casserole cuisine), every area has its own distinctive variations. Styles range from Hokkaido's salmon-based *ishikari-nabe* to Tokyo's *yanagawa-nabe*, which is made with *dojo* (an eel-like loach).

A favourite among locals – and something of an acquired taste for visitors – is *oden*. Made with *daikon* radish, potatoes, whole hard-boiled eggs, tofu, fish-paste patties and other ingredients, this hotpot, served with a dab of mustard, is one of the standard dishes served at *yatai* street stalls and convenience stores.

Above from far left: self-service from a revolving sushi bar; fresh *sashimi*.

Edomae Sushi
The concept of eating small patties of vinegared rice topped with cuts of raw seafood originated in the days of Edo and is still called Edomae sushi, because the seafood was caught in the bay in front of the city.

Left: *yakitori*, skewers of grilled chicken.

FOOD & DRINK 15

Above from left:
there is an etiquette to using chopsticks; freshly caught red snapper at Tsukiji Fish Market; a line of red lanterns indicates an *izakaya*.

In a Pickle
No meal is complete without a serving of *tsukemono* (pickles) to add nutrition and texture, cleanse the palate and assist digestion. They can be made from a wide variety of produce, including cucumber, turnip, cabbage and aubergine.

Grilled Food

Since Edo times, *unagi*, grilled eel served on a bed of rice, has had a reputation for giving energy during the summer, but it's just as delicious at other times of the year. Another grilled food is *yakitori*, skewers of chicken, often cooked over charcoal. Almost every part of the bird is eaten, from the breast to the heart. Gourmet versions can be had in upscale restaurants, but most people prefer the smoky street stalls.

Noodles

Noodles are the original Japanese fast food. *Soba* noodles are made with buckwheat flour – the best being *te-uchi*, freshly prepared and chopped by hand. *Zaru-soba* is a term for noodles served cold, accompanied by a dip made with soy sauce, *mirin* (sweet sake) and *katsuobushi* (shaved flakes of dried bonito), and flavoured with *wasabi* and thinly sliced spring onions. *Soba* can also be eaten with a hot broth, which may be topped with tempura, *sansai* (mountain greens), *wakame* seaweed or deep-fried tofu *(kitsune)*, or served with a raw egg cracked into it *(tsukimi)*. The classic dish, however, is *kamo-nanban*, in which the hot broth contains slices of duck meat and sliced leeks.

Other noodle types include chunky *udon*, made from white wheat flour, and the popular Chinese-style *ramen*, served in a hot soy-flavoured broth typically with pickled bamboo, chopped spring onion and slices of *cha-shu* (roast pork).

Kaiseki Ryori

Japan's culinary celebration of the seasons finds its ultimate expression in *kaiseki ryori*, a style of cooking derived from the banquets served as part of the tea ceremony. The taste and visual appeal of the dishes are created to ensure perfect harmony.

Kaiseki ryori is composed of numerous small courses, some little larger than a mouthful. They follow a prescribed order. First, there's a selection of appetisers; next, some *sashimi* and a clear soup are served; then follow dishes that have been grilled, seasoned with a thick dressing, simmered, steamed, deep-fried and dressed with vinegar.

Sake is served alongside the dishes, but never with the final course which consists of rice, a bowl of miso soup and a few pickles. Hot green tea is served alongside, and dessert is usually a small portion of fresh fruit.

Mind Your Manners

Impress Japanese guests with your knowledge of Japanese dining etiquette. It is bad manners to wave your chopsticks around, use them to point at someone, to spear food or to pull dishes forward. Do not pass food from your chopsticks to someone else's or even into their mouths. Japanese soups are sipped straight from the bowl. Pour soy sauce into the dipping saucer provided, not onto your food. It is polite to say *itadakimasu* ('I accept') before starting to eat and *gochisosama deshita* ('it was a banquet') after every meal.

Sweets

Japanese cuisine is not known for its sweets, but one type worth trying are *wagashi* (*'wa'* stands for things Japanese, *'gashi'* means sweets). *Wagashi* are mostly based on the *azuki* bean; this ingredient is mixed into *anko* (a sweet paste made with sugar), pressed into *anman* wheat buns and *mochi* rice flour shells, or processed into *yokan* (gelatin) and *higashi* (hard sweets). Confections are created according to the seasons; around the time of cherry-blossom viewing, *wagashiya* (sweet shops) sell cherry-flavoured treats, sometimes wrapped in cherry leaves.

COFFEE & TEA

The heart of Japan's coffee culture lies in its old-fashioned *kissaten*, like Kina *(see p.39)*, and its trendy European-style cafés, such as those along Omotesando *(see p.42)*. In recent years both have come under attack from cheaper generic chains like Doutor, Tully's and the ubiquitous Starbucks.

Tea is making something of a comeback – look for the chain Koots Green Tea (www.koots.jp), with branches in Roppongi and Harajuku. If you would like to sample a traditional tea ceremony the Four Seasons Chinzan-so, Imperial, New Otani and Okura hotels all have traditional rooms offering this experience.

ALCOHOLIC DRINKS

Beer is by far the most popular alcoholic beverage, the big four breweries – Asahi, Kirin, Sapporo and Suntory – each offering a wide range of beverages with new varieties each season. Microbreweries have also begun to take off, a good one being T.Y. Harbour Brewery *(see p.121)*.

Rice Wine

You should take the opportunity to try the Japanese rice wine sake (also known as *nihonshu*). It comes in tens of thousands of different brands, mainly in *amakuchi* (sweet) and *karakuchi* (dry) varieties. Tokyo-based sake expert John Gauntner's website www.esake.com has hundreds of reviews of Japanese sake brewers and sake bars, a 'Sake Knowledge' section and links to online sake shops in the US and elsewhere.

Fit for an Emperor
A good place to buy or sample Japanese sweets is Toraya (Akasaka 4-9-22, Minato-ku; tel: 3408 4121; www.toraya-group.co.jp; Mon–Fri 8.30am–8pm, Sat–Sun 8.30am–6pm), supplier of sweets to no less than the emperor himself.

Below: bottles of sake, Japanese rice wine.

FOOD & DRINK

SHOPPING

Tokyo is one of the world's premier shopping destinations. The options are immense, from centuries-old emporiums selling traditional crafts to prestigious department stores to cheerful novelty shops where everything is ¥100.

Opening Hours
Generally you will find stores open from 10am or 11am to 7pm or 8pm, with a few places staying open even later. Sunday trading is the norm, and if shops do close it will typically be on a Monday or Wednesday.

Below: cuddly toys at Kiddyland.

In a city where a good deal of status is attached to brand names, being seen with the right designer-label bag defines the shopper. Even if you don't know the brand, you can pretty much be assured of quality, a principle of Japanese manufacturing applied to everything from integrated circuits to the glaze on an earthenware pot. The Japanese take great pride in their work, a legacy of the old craft and trade guilds and the country's artisan traditions.

In Japan 'the customer is always right' becomes 'the customer is God'. Service here is an art; the wrapping, decorating and packaging of goods is all done with remarkable speed and dexterity, and staff will invariably be super-polite.

DEPARTMENT STORES AND MALLS

Department stores such as Isetan, Mitsukoshi and Takashimaya are regarded as institutions and like to think of themselves more as cultural centres than just marketplaces. You can find almost any product in these full-service stores and, if the weather is fine, you may be able to relax in the rooftop playground, beer garden or golf range. More sophisticated pleasures are provided by in-house art galleries.

The biggest change to Tokyo's shopping and leisure scene in recent years has been the emergence of state-of-the-art living complexes where visitors can be provided with everything they need for an entire day. Developments such as Roppongi Hills and Tokyo Midtown in Roppongi *(see p.37 and p.38)*, with their striking architecture and cultural facilities, have become destinations in their own right quite apart from the shopping opportunities they provide.

Even smaller malls such as the chic Ando Tadao-designed Omotesando Hills *(see p.44)* and Venus Fort in Odaiba *(see p.78)* are worth checking out, the latter having an artificial sky that cycles through dawn-to-dusk lighting effects.

ELECTRONICS

For electronics and hi-tech devices Akihabara, a couple of stops south of Ueno *(see p.59)* on the Yamanote line, offers many competitively priced stores such as Laox, which stocks duty-free overseas models, and Yodobashi Camera. You can also pick up good deals at Bic Camera, with its main store in Yurakucho opposite the Tokyo International Forum *(see p.33)* and other branches in Ikebukuro, Shinjuku and Shibuya.

FASHION

For high-end fashion and designer labels, head to Marunouchi and Ginza *(see p.32)*, where you will also find main branches of break-out retail successes such as Uniqlo (www.uniqlo.com/jp) and Muji (www.muji.net).

Japanese designers rule in Aoyama and the eclectic youth-orientated stores of Harajuku *(see p.42)*, as well as in nearby Shibuya *(see p.46)*. Also well worth a browse are the trendy boutiques of Daikanyama and Naka-Meguro, both a train or subway stop away from Shibuya and Ebisu respectively.

Another dressing-up option is the so-called 'Fashion Building'. Tokyo has hundreds of these multi-floored malls that rent space to different boutiques to showcase their latest collections; they include places like La Foret (www.laforet.ne.jp) in Harajuku and Shibuya's 109 Building.

TRADITIONAL CRAFTS

If you are in the market for traditional crafts, then head to Asakusa *(see p.66)*. While here you can also explore a wide range of kitchen and tableware available in nearby Kappabashi. Rounding out this northeastern Tokyo retail experience is Ueno, where the Ameya Yokocho market area is good for cheap food, cosmetics, clothing and toys *(see p.61)*. Also good for craft souvenirs are Oriental Bazaar in Harajuku *(see p.44)* and Ito-ya in Ginza *(see p.35)*.

SHOPPING RULES

Although there are some exceptions, prices in Tokyo are generally fixed and non-negotiable. Shops accepting overseas credit cards remain relatively rare, although you shouldn't have a problem in the main department stores. Large department stores are usually happy to refund the 5 percent consumption tax to foreign customers who purchase goods over ¥10,000, but you will have to produce your passport.

Above from far left: fashion boutique in Shibuya; geisha design on chinaware at the Oriental Bazaar.

Bowing to Customers
The morning ritual (usually at 10am) when a department store opens its doors is well worth attending. Uniformed staff, immaculately turned out, stand at the main entrance and at the top of the escalators, bowing to each customer in turn.

Left: Venus Fort mall in Odaiba.

SHOPPING 19

SPORTS & ENTERTAINMENT

Baseball is what gets most Tokyo sports fans excited, but there are also chances to watch sumo and martial arts in the capital. Similarly, when it comes to performing arts, the city provides an eclectic mix of the traditional and the contemporary.

SUMO

Steeped in Shinto rituals, the national sport of sumo has been around for at least 2,000 years. Allegations of match-fixing and bad behaviour by wrestlers have tainted the sport in recent years, but it still commands a strong following, and witnessing a tournament may well be a highlight of your trip to Japan.

Matches between wrestlers (called *rikishi*), who can weigh up to and over 68kg (150lbs), were traditionally held at shrines such as Yasukuni-jinja *(see p.28)* where they still occasionally take place. They are punctuated by ritual stomping to drive evil spirits from the ring, and salt-throwing for purification.

The apprenticeship of a *rikishi* is long and harsh. Only when the wrestler makes it to the higher ranks of *ozeki* or rarely achieved *yokozuna* (grand champion) does life become easier. Those in the lower ranks become servants of the *ozeki* or *yokozuna*, running errands and scrubbing backs.

Three of sumo's six annual 15-day tournaments occur at Tokyo's National Sumo Stadium *(see p.73)* in January, May and September. In downtimes you can visit sumo stables to observe wrestlers' morning practice sessions.

BASEBALL

Some of Japan's top *yakkyu* (baseball) stars have moved to the US Major Leagues, but a game at either the Tokyo Dome (near Korakuen Station; www.tokyo-dome.co.jp), home ground of the Yomuri Giants, or Jingu Stadium (near Gaienmae Station), base for the Yakult Swallows, demonstrates how the Japanese have made the sport their own.

Japan's 'second national sport' (but top spectator sport) maintains its appeal among the older generation. Younger Japanese seem less keen, although the Major League success of young players such as Ichiro Suzuki, Daisuke Matsuzaka (who currently plays for the Boston Red Sox) and others is changing that. The season runs from April to October, culminating in the best-of-seven Japan Series between the pennant winners of the two leagues.

Martial Arts
Judo, karate, aikido, *kyudo* (archery) and *kendo* (fencing) all have regular championships or demonstration events, which are usually held at the Nippon Budokan *(see p.30)*.

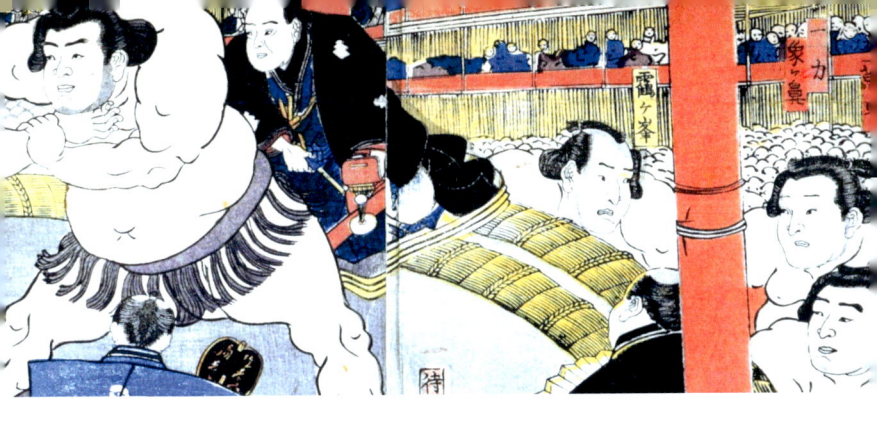

FOOTBALL

The 2002 World Cup gave a major boost to the popularity of football (soccer) in Japan. The J-League (www.j-league.or.jp) football season runs from March to October, with a special Emperor's Cup event in December. Regular J-League games are played at the National Stadium, near Sendagaya Station, as well as international fixtures. The capital's two top teams, FC Tokyo and Tokyo Verdy, play at the new Ajinomoto Stadium in Chofu City, western Tokyo.

THEATRE AND DANCE

Tokyo offers an interesting range of performing arts. From Japanese antiquity there is the entrancing masked stillness of *noh*, the masterful puppetry of *bunraku* and the garish stylisation of *kabuki*. Or there are outstanding performance halls for top-notch Western-style musicals, ballet and contemporary dance. Then there is avant-garde *butoh* or experimental theatre at one of Tokyo's tiny black-box venues.

Bunraku

The adult puppet theatre of *bunraku* is an art dating back to the 7th century, when itinerant Chinese and Korean performers presented semi-religious puppet plays. As with *kabuki* and *noh*, the plays deal with themes such as revenge and sacrifice, love and rejection, reincarnation and futility.

Each major puppet is manipulated by three operators, a logistic marvel in itself. In theory, the audience does not notice all the shuffling of the black-clad professional puppeteers, concentrating instead on the puppets, which are roughly one-third of the size of a human. The real tour de force, though, are the narrators – the *gidayu* performers – who speak, gesture and weep from a kneeling position at stage left.

Kabuki

In Japanese *kabuki* translates as 'song-dance skill', with no mention of theatre, although the performances themselves are highly stylised and theatrical. In the early 16th century the word *kabuki* meant 'avant-garde' and referred to all-female performances, often of a licentious nature. The

Above: National Sumo Stadium mural.

Below: you can catch baseball games at the Tokyo Dome.

SPORTS & ENTERTAINMENT

National Theatre

The premier venue for Japan's traditional performing arts, including *kabuki*, *bunraku* and imperial court music and dance, is the National Theatre (4-1 Hayabusa-cho, Chiyoda-ku; tel: 3265 7411 for enquiries; tel: 3230 3000 for reservations; www.ntj.jac.go.jp; station: Hanzamon).

Listings

For a selection of bars, live-music venues and clubs, see pp.120–3. You can also pick up a free copy of the weekly listings magazine *Metropolis* (http://metropolis.co.jp) each Friday at major hotels, restaurants, bars and shops where foreigners gather.

Tokugawa shogunate banned female performers in 1629. This started the all-male tradition that continues today; actresses are only allowed for certain special events.

The main *kabuki* theatres are the Kabuki-za *(see p.35)*, the Shimbashi Embujo (6-12-2 Ginza, Chuo-ku; tel: 3541 2600; station: Shimbashi) and the National Theatre *(see margin)*. Most programmes span three or four hours, with generous intervals for tea-drinking and socialising; for most visitors a single act or around an hour or so will be sufficient to get a taste.

Noh

This minimalist theatre is a development from early temple plays. Aristocratic patronage demanded esoteric poetry, sophisticated language and a refined simplicity of movement, precisely what you see six centuries later. It is difficult to describe *noh* – words like 'ethereal', 'inaccessible' and 'subtle' spring to mind. Fortunately, some English translations are available. Catch *noh* performances at the National Noh Theatre (4-18-1 Sendagaya, Shibuya-ku; tel: 3423 1331; www.ntj.jac.go.jp; station: Sendagaya).

Western-Style Theatre

Translations of foreign plays and musicals, imported from London and New York, are very popular and range from Chekhov to *Cats*. Most are performed in Japanese by Japanese dancers and singers. Performances can be a mixed experience.

For a very Japanese take on musical theatre, attend a performance by the Takarazuka Revue (http://kageki.hankyu.co.jp), an all-female song-and-dance extravaganza. It is unashamedly flamboyant and romantic, with gorgeous costumes. Watched mainly by middle-aged housewives and young women, the shows are held at the Takurazuka Theatre opposite the Imperial Hotel *(see p.35)*.

Tokyo also offers a lively experimental theatre scene, known as the *shogekijo* ('little theatre') movement. Much of the activity centres on the counterculture district of Shimokitazawa, west of Shibuya, where there are many small venues.

Classical Music and Ballet

A dedicated following exists for classical music and ballet, with performances by domestic companies at venues such as Tokyo Opera City and the New National Theatre *(see p.52)* on the western side of Shinjuku, and Bunkamura's Orchard Hall *(see p.48)* in Shibuya.

Keep an eye out for performances by the celebrated Tokyo-based Asami Maki Ballet (www.ambt.jp) and the K-Ballet Company; the latter is headed up by Tetsuya Kumakawa, who has also performed with the UK's Royal Ballet.

Contemporary Dance

Tokyo has a fervent audience for boldly experimental dance performances, which can involve innovative multi-media. Performances are held at Session House (158 Yaraicho, Shinjuku-ku; tel: 3266 0461; station: Kagurazaka), Aoyama Theatre (5-53-1 Jingumae, Shibuya-ku; tel: 3797 5678; www.aoyama.org; station: Omotesando) and the New National Theatre.

Butoh

Originally called a 'dance of darkness', *butoh* strives not for beauty and physical grace, but to depict the inhumanity and discord of existence, with cathartic results for the audience. This internationally renowned avant-garde dance form is becoming more widely accepted in its home country. The best place to see *butoh* is at the cosy Azabu Die Pratze (1-26-6 Higashi-Azabu, Minato-ku; tel: 5545 1385) near Tokyo Tower.

POPULAR MUSIC

Japanese devotion to music is legendary, and as the capital of the world's second-biggest music market, Tokyo is at the centre of it. From its vast stadiums to its smoky dives, from ancient sounds to the cutting edge, Tokyo boasts a lifetime's worth of musical experience any night of the week; for suggestions of venues to check out, *see pp. 122–3*. With an increasing number of bands touring Tokyo and more foreign musicians choosing to make it their home, its music scene is becoming progressively more international. CD and vinyl buffs can also indulge in the world's most diverse market for record-shopping.

Above from far left: poster advertising a *kabuki* performance; music fans checking out some vinyl.

Otaku Culture

Otaku – originally a derogatory term for people with pathologically obsessive interests in *anime* (Japanese animation) and *manga* (Japanese comics) – has now become synonymous with Japanese cool as well as an economy reportedly worth US$3.5 billion.

As well as being home to hundreds of electronics and software shops, Akihabara (*Akiba* to the faithful) is the first place many fans head to find maid cafés (where waitresses dress up in costumes), *cosplay* hobby outlets (for dressing up as a favourite *anime* character) and the like. Also here is the Tokyo Anime Centre (www.animecenter.jp), a showroom for the newest and best-known *anime*, with a screening room, exhibition galleries, shop and studio where visitors can listen to actors recording dialogue.

In Tokyo's western suburbs is the Ghibli Museum (www.ghibli-museum.jp), celebrating the animated movies of Studio Ghibli, such as Hayao Miyazaki's *Spirited Away*. The store Mandarake (www.mandarake.co.jp) is a temple for *manga* and *anime* fanatics, with branches in Nakano and Shibuya.

HISTORY: KEY DATES

Tokyo's rise from humble fishing village to contemporary economic powerhouse stretches back over a millennium, during which time it has survived practically the worst that nature and mankind could throw at it.

PRE-EDO PERIODS

628AD Senso-ji (Asakusa Kannon) is founded after two brothers discover a golden statue of the bodhisattva Kannon in their fishing nets.
1180 The first recorded use of the name Edo (meaning 'Rivergate') for the area later to become Tokyo.
1457 Ota Dokan, the poet and monk celebrated as Tokyo's founder, builds a castle at Edo. First land-reclamation project.
1590 Tokugawa Ieyasu begins construction of a new fortress on site of Ota Dokan's old castle.

EDO PERIOD (1603–1868)

1603 The beginning of the 265-year rule of the Tokugawa dynasty, governing from their military base at Edo.
1657 The Furisode (Long Sleeves) Fire destroys most of the city and kills a quarter of Edo's inhabitants.
1707 Ash covers Edo after an eruption of Mount Fuji.
1742 Roughly 4,000 die in Edo after a series of floods and storms.
1780 The city's population reaches 1.3 million. Edo is probably the largest city in the world at this time.
1853 Commodore Matthew Perry's Black Ships appear in Tokyo Bay, signalling the end of Japan's 250-year isolation from outside world.
1855 A major earthquake hits Edo, killing over 7,000 residents and destroying much of the Shitamachi area.

MEIJI PERIOD (1868–1912)

1868 Edo is renamed Tokyo.
1869 The emperor Meiji moves to Tokyo, which becomes the new capital and seat of government.

1872	Japan's first railway line begins service from Yokohama to Shimbashi.
1882	The Bank of Japan is established in Nihonbashi district.
1890	The first sitting of the Imperial Diet (legislative assembly) takes place.
1894	Marunouchi becomes the site of a European-style business quarter known as 'London Town'.
1903	Asakusa becomes home to Japan's first permanent cinema.

Above from far left: 17th-century woodblock print of the bridge Nihombashi; destruction wrought by the Great Kanto Earthquake.

TAISHO & SHOWA PERIODS (1912–89)

1920	Meiji-jingu is constructed.
1922	The Imperial Hotel, designed by Frank Lloyd Wright, opens in Hibiya.
1923	The Great Kanto Earthquake leaves over 100,000 people dead, and a quarter of the city is wiped out in the fire of the aftermath.
1927	A subway, the first in Asia, is completed between Asakusa and Ueno.
1932	Tokyo's city limits are expanded to its current 23 wards.
1945	American B-29s fire-bomb the city. Over half the city is destroyed and 100,000 civilians die.
1945–52	American occupation years. General McArthur sets up headquarters in Tokyo. Post-war national reconstruction begins.
1955	The Liberal Democratic Party is formed and wins the general election. It has been the ruling party of Japan ever since.
1964	The city hosts the Olympics, an event of immense prestige.

HEISEI PERIOD (1989–)

1989	The death of Emperor Hirohito at the Imperial Palace ushers in the new emperor Akihito and the Heisei era.
1990	The bubble economy bursts, triggering a slump in Tokyo land prices.
1991	The Kenzo Tange-designed Tokyo Municipal Government Office opens.
1995	Members of the Aum Shinrikyo cult release sarin gas in a commuter train, killing 12 and injuring thousands.
1999	Ishihara Shintaro, an outspoken nationalist, is elected as Tokyo governor.
2002	The Fifa World Cup final is played in Tokyo following Japan and Korea's co-hosting of football tournament.
2003	The opening of the Roppongi Hills complex heralds the reinvention of the nightlife district into a chic shopping and arts hub.
2007	Ishihara is re-elected for a third consecutive term.
2008	The Fukutoshin line, the 13th on the city's metro, goes into operation.

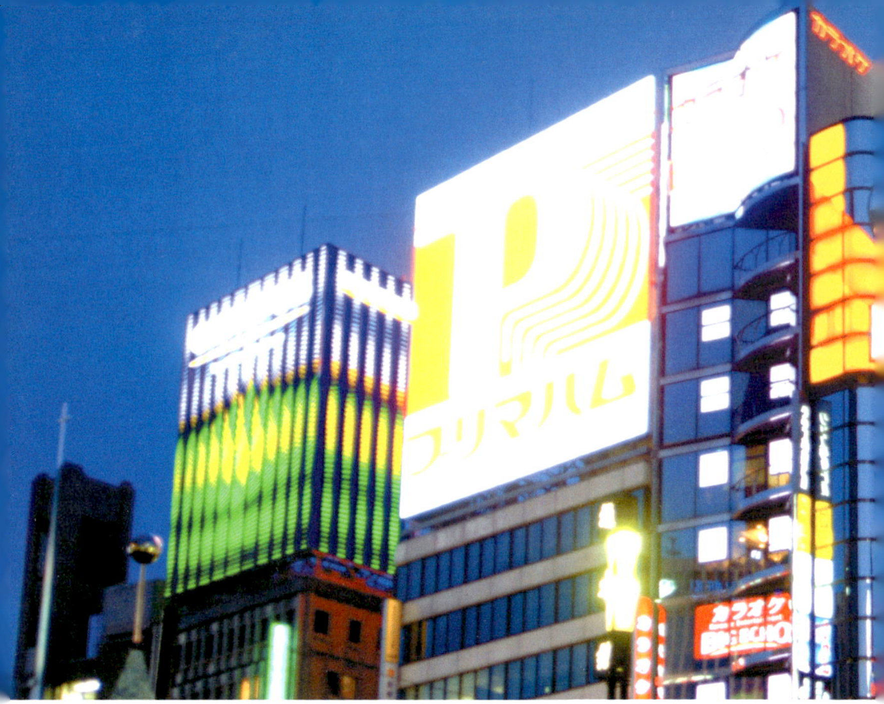
プリマハム
カラオケ

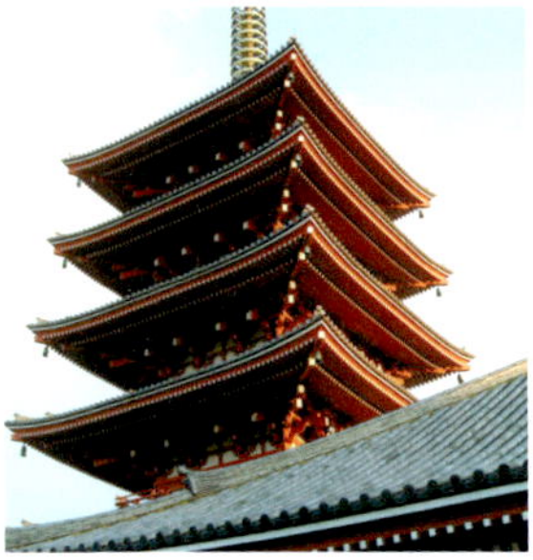

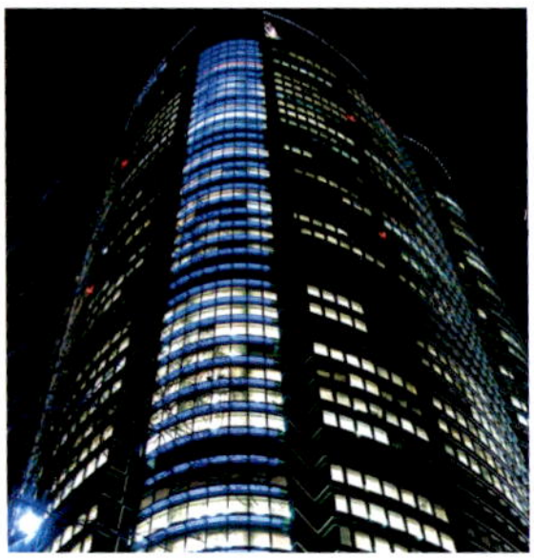

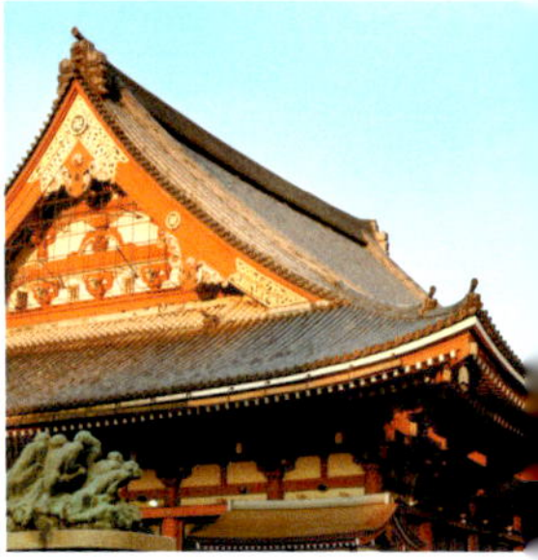

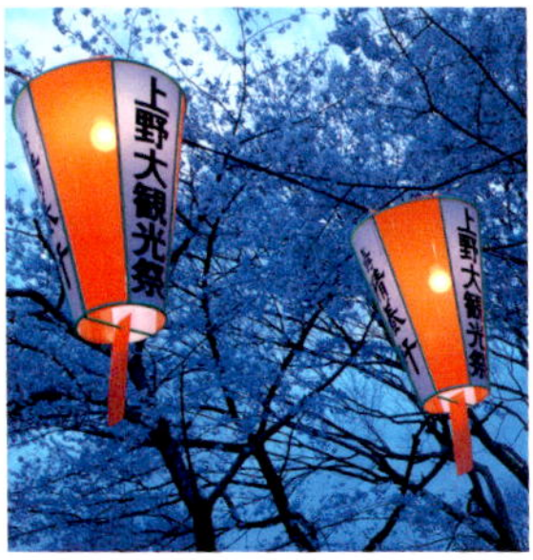
上野大観光祭
上野大観光祭

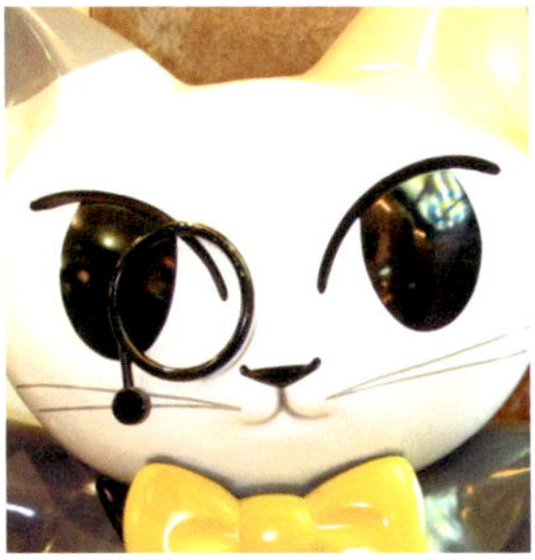

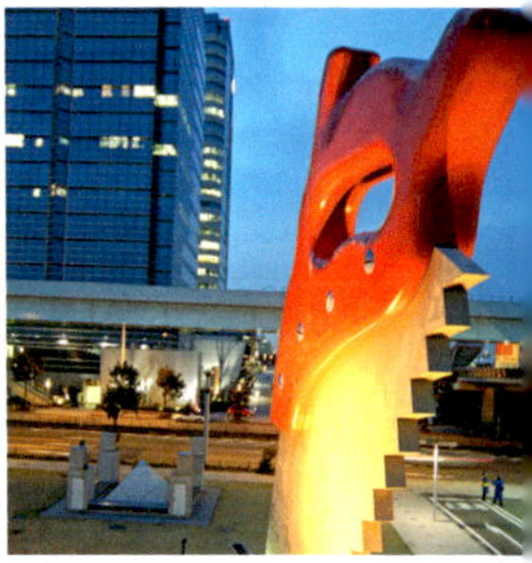

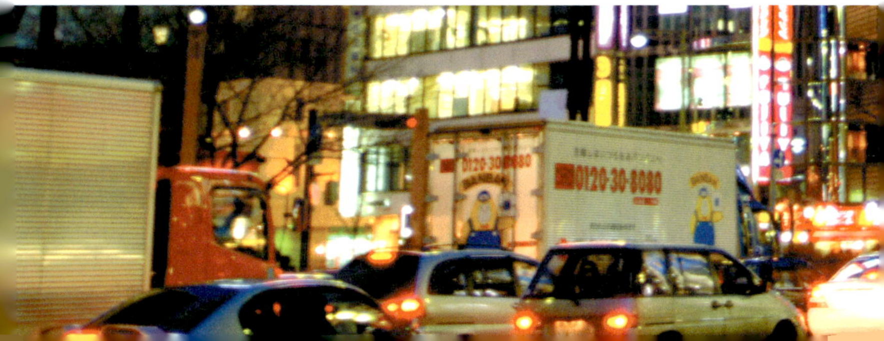
0120-30-8080

WALKS & TOURS

1.	The Imperial Palace & Around	28	9.	Asakusa	66
2.	Marunouchi & Ginza	32	10.	Fukagawa & Ryogoku	70
3.	Roppongi & Akasaka	36	11.	Tsukiji & Tsukudajima	74
4.	Aoyama & Harajuku	42	12.	Odaiba	78
5.	Shibuya & Ebisu	46	13.	Kawagoe	80
6.	Shinjuku	50	14.	Kamakura & Enoshima	84
7.	Yanaka & Ueno	56	15.	Hakone	88
8.	Ikebukuro & Mejirodai	62	16.	Nikko	92

THE IMPERIAL PALACE & AROUND

After a visit to Tokyo's most controversial shrine, stroll through the peaceful Imperial Palace grounds, taking in a couple of interesting art museums and finishing up at the city's first European-style park.

Yasukuni Festivals
There are hundreds of cherry trees in Yasukuni's grounds, making this a prime spot for *hanami* (cherry-blossom viewing) in spring. Festivals to entertain the spirits of the dead are also held in the shrine grounds at the end of April and mid-October.

DISTANCE 5km (3 miles)
TIME A half day
START Kudanshita Station
END Hibiya Station
POINTS TO NOTE
The Imperial Palace East Garden is closed on Mondays and Fridays. Volunteers offer a free two-hour walking tour around the Imperial Palace grounds on Saturdays at 1pm (meet at the gate of the Central Marunouchi entrance in Tokyo Station; http://freewalkingtour.org).

Japan's War Dead

Before an important battle, soldiers sometimes exchanged the words, 'Let us meet at Yasukuni', meaning the place where their spirits would be honoured. In 1979 several Class-A war criminals were enshrined here, outraging Japan's neighbours. Every 15 August – the anniversary of the country's defeat in World War II – the controversy erupts afresh, when a ceremony is held at Yasukuni. Japan's post-war constitution renounces both militarism and state-sponsored religion, so cabinet members who attend are asked whether they are there as private individuals or public figures.

At the heart of the buzzing metropolis, the Imperial Palace, home to the world's oldest monarchy, stands amid the grounds of the once formidable Edo Castle. Tokyo's rise began here in 1590, when the first shogun, Tokugawa Ieyasu, chose the site as his new headquarters. When the castle was completed in 1640, it was the largest in the world, a fact you can ponder as you stroll through the spacious grounds on your way to Hibiya Park.

YASUKUNI-JINJA

From Kudanshita Station, walk uphill towards the huge steel *torii* gate marking the entrance to **Yasukuni-jinja** ❶ (www.yasukuni.or.jp). Built to enshrine the remains of around 2.5 million war dead, this controversial Shinto shrine *(see left)* was completed in 1869. The original gate was requisitioned and melted to make armaments in 1943. To the rear, there is a pretty ornamental garden with a teahouse and an adjacent sumo ring where bouts are held during the shrine's spring festival.

Yushukan

Yasukuni's fascinating museum, **Yushukan** ❷ (daily Apr–Sept 9am–5.30pm, Oct–Mar 9am–5pm; charge), houses samurai costumes, faded photos, letters from the front and other reminders of Japan's tragic military past. Look out for the *kaiten*, a human suicide torpedo.

KITANOMARU PARK

Cross busy Yasukuni-dori to reach **Tayasu-mon** ❸, the entrance gate to **Kitanomaru Park** (Kitanomaru-koen). The former home of the Imperial Guard is now a wooded area with nature trails and some interesting museums.

Above from far left: Imperial Palace; flowers in the East Garden; Yasukuni-jinja.

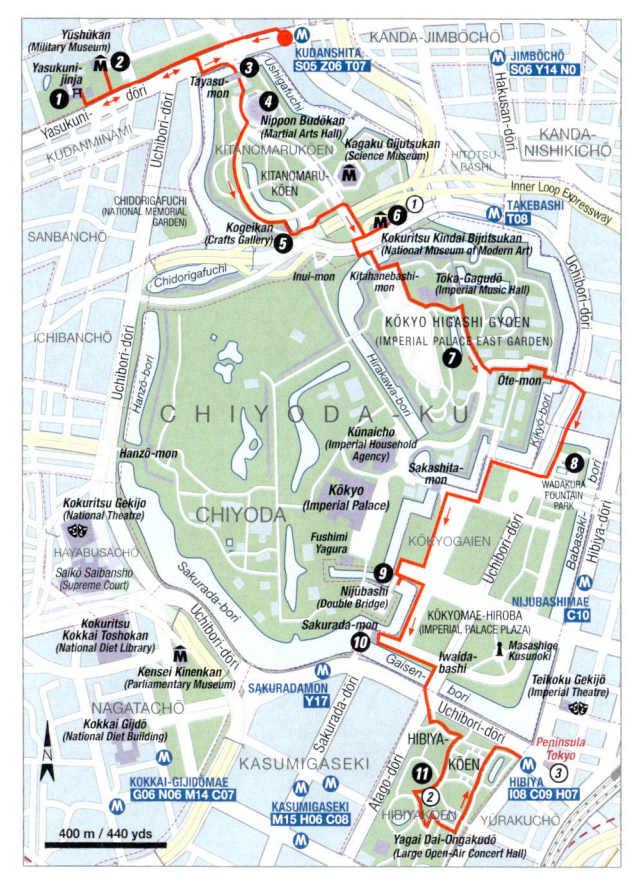

Witness to History

The Imperial Palace Plaza has witnessed some momentous scenes of recent history. Survivors of the Great Kanto Earthquake gathered here in 1923, and in August 1945 several members of Japan's officer corps committed *seppuku* (ritual suicide) here, in order, it is said, to atone for their failure in World War II. In the 1950s and 60s student radicals and workers rallied at the plaza to take part in sometimes violent demonstrations.

Nippon Budokan

Walk south and the outline of the martial arts hall **Nippon Budokan** ❹ (tel: 3216 5100; ww.nipponbudokan.or.jp), built for the 1964 Olympics, will come into view. The design of this striking octagonal hall, with a curving roof and what looks like a golden top-knot, is based on that of the Horyu-ji Buddhist temple's Hall of Dreams near the ancient city of Nara (southwest of Tokyo). Concerts, exhibitions and tournaments of karate, archery, judo and Japanese fencing are held here.

Crafts Gallery

Continue through the park, heading to the right to reach the rewarding **Crafts Gallery** ❺ (Kogeikan; tel: 5777 8600; www.momat.go.jp; Tue–Sun 10am–5pm; charge), which is housed in a handsome Gothic Revival-style red-brick building, erected in 1910 to accommodate the old Imperial Palace Guard. Many of the exhibits, notably ceramic items, textiles and lacquerware, are the work of craftsmen honoured as 'Living National Treasures'.

National Museum of Modern Art

The Crafts Gallery is an annexe of the nearby **National Museum of Modern Art** ❻ (Kokuritsu Kindai Bijutsukan; tel: 5777 8600; www.momat.go.jp; Tue–Thur, Sun 10am–5pm, Fri 10am–8pm; charge). Besides an impressive display of paintings and sculptures by Japanese artists from the Meiji era to the present, the museum also has a few works by foreign artists such as Picasso. **Aqua**, see ❶, is the museum's stylish restaurant and café.

AROUND THE IMPERIAL PALACE EAST GARDEN

Passing over the highway and a section of the old castle moat, walk through the Kitahanebashi-mon gate to enter the **Imperial Palace East Garden** ❼ (Kokyo Higashi Gyoen; Tue–Thur, Sat–Sun 9am–4pm; free). This ornamental garden, with its inner circle of moats, was the site of Edo's original five-tiered keep. The keep burnt down in a major fire that swept

Food and Drink

① AQUA
National Museum of Modern Art, 3-1 Kitanomaru-koen, Chiyoda-ku; tel: 5777 8600; Tue–Sun 10am–5pm and 7–9pm; station: Takebashi; ¥¥
A giant sculpture by Japanese-American artist Isamu Noguchi stands outside this pleasant contemporary restaurant with an outdoor terrace. Dishes served include roast chicken and sautéed salmon.

② MATSUMOTORO
1-2 Hibiya-koen, Chiyoda-ku; tel: 3503 1451; daily 10am–9pm; station: Hibiya; ¥¥
In the centre of Hibiya Park, try Japanese takes on Western dishes (a style known as *yoshoku*) or relax over afternoon tea.

③ HEI FUNG TERRACE
The Peninsula Tokyo, 1-8-1 Yurakucho, Chiyoda-ku; tel: 6270 2738; daily 11.30am–2.30pm, 6–10pm; station: Hibiya; ¥¥¥
Enjoy a Chinese feast at this excellent restaurant specialising in Cantonese cuisine.

Edo in 1657. The heat was apparently so intense that it melted all the gold reserves kept in the keep's vault. Only its sturdy stone base survives, but it is worth climbing this to get a view of the surroundings, including the mosaic-decorated **Imperial Music Hall** (Toka-Gagudo).

The walls of the inner moat have fared better. Huge blocks were cut from great slabs of stone brought by ship from Izu, 80km (50 miles) away. More than 100 men were needed to load the rocks onto sledges and haul them to the castle. Seaweed was laid along the path to aid their progress.

Wadakura Fountain Park

Leave the garden through Ote Gate (Ote-mon), an impressive replica of the original main gate, and step into the precincts of the Outer Garden, now known as the **Imperial Palace Plaza** (Kokyomae Hiroba). The former gardens, planted with some 2,000 Japanese black pine trees and lawns in 1899, are split by wide Uchibori-dori. In the plaza's northeastern corner is the **Wadakura Fountain Park** ❽, built to celebrate the royal wedding of the emperor and empress in 1961, and refurbished on the occasion of their son's marriage in 1995.

Nijubashi

Continue south across the plaza to have your photograph taken against the picturesque backdrop of **Nijubashi** ❾, the Double Layer Bridge, with the graceful outline of the Fushimi Turret (Fushimi Yagura), and perhaps a swan or two gliding under the willow trees of the outer moat.

Follow the moat south to find **Sakurada-mon** ❿, dating from 1620, the largest of the remaining gates of Edo Castle. Although damaged by the Great Kanto Earthquake of 1923, the gate was rebuilt and is designated an 'Important Cultural Asset'.

HIBIYA PARK

Exit the Imperial Palace Plaza at the Iwaida Bridge (Iwaida-bashi) over the Gaisen Moat (Gaisen-bori). Cross the highway and enter **Hibiya Park** ⓫ (Hibiya-koen) on your left. This 16ha (41-acre) former parade ground was restyled as Japan's first Western-style park in 1903. It remains a curious mixture of Meiji-period Japanese and European landscaping, with an original wisteria trellis, crane fountain and a Japanese garden tucked into the southwestern corner, complete with stone lanterns and a pond.

Among the several places to eat here, the most pleasant is **Matsumo-toro**, see ❷. Alternatively, exit the park at its northeastern corner and cross the road to the Peninsula Tokyo hotel for afternoon tea in its lobby or lunch at its Chinese restaurant, **Hei Fung Terrace**, see ❸.

Above from far left: pine trees by one of the palace moats; statue of Kusunoki Masashige, a 14th-century samurai, in the Imperial Palace Plaza; the red-brick Crafts Gallery.

Palace Tours

The only time the general public is allowed to see the exterior of the Imperial Palace (Kokyo) is on 23 December (the emperor's birthday) and 2 January, when the emperor and other key members of the imperial family stand on a balcony in front of the reception building and wave to thousands of well-wishers. Avoid the crowds by signing up for a free place on one of the two official daily tours into the inner sanctum; see www.kunaicho.go.jp for details.

IMPERIAL PALACE EAST GARDEN

MARUNOUCHI & GINZA

There's more to the revitalised business and shopping districts of Marunouchi and Ginza than retail therapy, as you will discover on this walk along the grid-like streets to the east of the Imperial Palace.

> **DISTANCE** 5km (3 miles)
> **TIME** A half day
> **START/END** Hibiya Station
> **POINTS TO NOTE**
> This route follows on from the Imperial Palace walk *(see p.28)*. It is good to start in the late afternoon, so you can see Ginza lit up at night.

Both Marunouchi and Ginza are synonymous with expensive chic; against strong competition from other quarters they retain their charm, especially for the well-heeled, middle-aged shopper. The boutiques lining Marunouchi's Naka-dori (Tokyo's Rodeo Drive) or Ginza's Chuo-dori (its Fifth Avenue) are a roll call of designer labels, from Armani to Louis Vuitton. But there are also cultural treasures here, plus prime examples of heritage and contemporary architecture.

A Ginza Stroll
Ginza's Chuo-dori from 1-chome to 8-chome is closed to traffic Sat 2–6pm and Sun noon–5pm, when it becomes a pleasant pedestrian zone where you can enjoy a traditional *Gin-bura* (Ginza stroll), an expression coined in the 19th century.

MARUNOUCHI

It's a long time since Marunouchi lived up to its name – 'within the castle walls'. The opening of Tokyo Station in 1914 put it on the modern map, and today it is enjoying a renaissance as the landowner Mitsubishi redevelops the area.

Naka-dori
Once an anonymous street of office buildings, **Naka-dori** ❶ has blossomed into a sophisticated shopping strip. Start exploring it from the rear entrance of the **Peninsula Tokyo** *(see p.108)*, taking a moment to look up to your left just after you pass the first cross-street; poised at the hotel's corner is a gargoyle.

Idemitsu Museum of Art
Head up Naka-dori one more block and turn left to reach the **Idemitsu Museum of Art** ❷ (Idemitsu Bijutsukan; tel: 5777 8600; www.idemitsu.co.jp/museum; Tue–Thur, Sat–Sun 10am–5pm; charge), hidden away on the ninth floor of the same building as the Imperial Theatre. This is one of Tokyo's best private museums, housing a superb collection of Japanese ceramics, *ukiyo-e* woodblock prints,

Food and Drink
① **PÂTISSERIE SADAHARU AOKI**
3-4-1 Marunouchi, Chiyoda-ku; tel: 5293 2800; www.sadaharuaoki.com; daily 11am–9pm; station: Yurakucho; ¥
Pastry chef Sadaharu Aoki is the toast of Paris for his divine sweet creations. Sample éclairs, macaroons and filled croissants here at his first Tokyo 'boutique'.

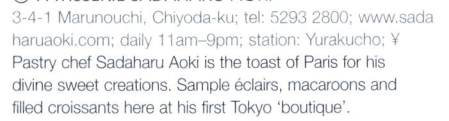

folding screens, exquisite Momoyama and early Edo-period gold-leaf genre paintings, and the 15th-century monochrome paintings of the Zen monk Sesshu. Its lounge provides a panoramic view of the Imperial Palace.

Tokyo International Forum

Return to and cross Naka-dori, and continue for one more block, passing **Pâtisserie Sadaharu AOKI**, see ①①, to reach the striking **Tokyo International Forum** ❸ (tel: 5221 9000; www.t-i-forum.co.jp). Opened in 1997, the exhibition hall and theatre complex is the work of New York-based designer Rafael Vinoly. To get a bird's-eye view, go up to the seventh floor, where skywalks criss-cross the middle of a curving 60m (190ft) high glass atrium shaped like a ship's hull.

Mitsubishi Ichigokan Museum

Return to Naka-dori to find the **Mitsubishi Ichigokan Museum** ❹ (http://mimt.jp; charge). Set to open

Above from far left: shoppers in Ginza; inside Tokyo International Forum.

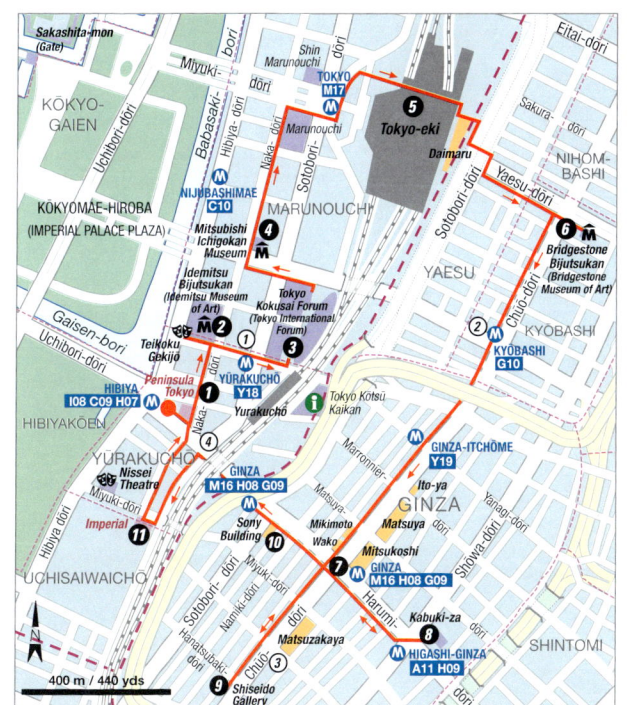

Antiques Market
The Oedo Antiques Market (http://antique-market.jp) is held in the central atrium of the Tokyo International Forum on the 1st and 3rd Sundays of the month.

IDEMITSU MUSEUM OF ART 33

Above from left: Ginza chic; Paul Cézanne at the Bridgestone Museum of Art; Tokyo Station.

in April 2010, this art museum will focus on works from the mid-18th to 20th centuries. It is housed in a meticulous replica of the handsome 1894 red-brick office building – the first in the area – designed by Josiah Conder *(see margin, right)*.

Tokyo Station

Continue to the intersection of Naka-dori and broad Miyuki-dori, flanked by the high-rise Marunouchi and Shin-Marunouchi buildings. Turn right to face the handsome brick façade of **Tokyo Station** ❺. This fine example of Taisho-era Western architecture, designed by Tatsuno Kingo, a former student of Conder, is undergoing a major renovation set to finish in 2011, when many of the building's original features, including a hotel, will be restored.

BRIDGESTONE MUSEUM OF ART

Negotiate the pedestrian corridor beneath the station's tracks that leads from the Marunouchi to the Yaesu side of the building, emerging beside Daimaru department store facing Yaesu-dori. Walk two blocks east to the intersection with Chuo-dori and the **Bridgestone Museum of Art** ❻ (Bridgestone Bijutsukan; 1-10-1 Kyobashi, Chuo-ku; tel: 3563 0241; www.bridgestone-museum.gr.jp; Tue–Sat 10am–8pm, Sun and hols 10am–6pm; charge). The tyre manufacturer's art collection is composed mainly of Impressionists' works, but there are also early 20th-century painters and post-Meiji-era Japanese artists here, as well as sculptures.

Chocolate Boost

Continue south down Chuo-dori towards Kyobashi subway station; nearby you can grab an energy boost from **100% Chocolate Café**, see ②, before tackling the next boutique-and-department-store-studded stretch of the street.

Food and Drink

② 100% CHOCOLATE CAFÉ
2-4-16 Kyobashi, Chuo-ku; tel: 3237 3184; www.choco-cafe.jp; Mon–Fri 8am–8pm, Sat–Sun 11am–7pm; station: Kyobashi; ¥
Local chocolate-maker Meiji offers chocoholic heaven at this café specialising in drinks and confections made from the cocoa bean. The decor is by one of Tokyo's trendiest designers.

③ LION BEER HALL
7-9-20 Ginza, Chuo-ku; tel: 3571 2590; www.ginzalion.jp; Mon–Sat 11.30am–11pm, Sun 11.30am–10pm; station: Ginza; ¥¥
Worth dropping by, if only to marvel at the ground-floor beer hall's vaulted ceiling and mosaic-lined decor. Brewery Sapporo's beers are accompanied by Germanic-style sausages and the like.

④ SHIN-HINOMOTO
2-4-4 Yurakucho, Chiyoda-ku; tel: 3214 8021; Mon–Sat 5pm–midnight; stations: Yurakucho or Hibiya; ¥¥
A noisy, friendly, no-nonsense *izakaya* (tavern) built under the railway tracks, serving fresh seafood at reasonable prices. English-speaking.

GINZA

Two of the area's best-known retail landmarks stand on the corner of the **Ginza 4-chome crossing** ❼. The exclusive department store **Wako**, owned by the watch company Seiko, is housed in one of the few buildings to have survived the World War II air raids that flattened Ginza; it dates back to 1932. Across the road is **Mitsukoshi**, a top city department store. Also close by are **Mikimoto**, selling cultured pearls, and **Ito-ya**, a superb paper and stationery store.

Kabuki-za

From Ginza 4-chome head southeast along Harumi-dori for several blocks to reach the opulent exterior of **Kabuki-za** ❽ (4-12-15 Ginza, Chuo-ku; tel: 5565 6000; www.kabuki-za.co.jp; due to close in April 2010, *see right*). Here colourful and highly stylised *kabuki* dramas, combining music, dance and singing, are staged twice a day (usually starting at 11am and 4.30pm) during the first three weeks of the month – catching at least one act is recommended. Founded in 1889 and rebuilt in 1924, the theatre sports an elaborate roof and highly decorative porch.

Shiseido Gallery

Ginza is also well known for its many small art galleries. A good one to head to is the **Shiseido Gallery** ❾ (8-8-3 Ginza, Chuo-ku; tel: 3572 3901; www.shiseido.co.jp/gallery/html; Tue–Sat 11am–7pm, Sun and hols 11am–6pm; free) in the basement of Shiseido Parlour, a cosmetics boutique. It features experimental art by Japanese and foreign artists. On the way there or back along Chuo-dori you will pass the **Lion Beer Hall**, see ⓘ③; pop in to admire its attractive interior design.

Sony Building

Return to Ginza 4-chome and turn left, heading along Harumi-dori past more luxury boutiques to the **Sony Building** ❿ (tel: 3573 2371; www.sonybuilding.jp; daily 11am–7pm), six floors stuffed with the latest techno-wizardry just waiting to be tried out.

OLD IMPERIAL BAR

Continue under the raised expressway and the railway tracks, keeping an eye out for Shinkansen (bullet trains). You will eventually arrive back where you started above Hibiya Station. To round off, there are a couple of choices. You could turn left and follow the track until you reach the junction with Miyuki-dori where to the right is the rear of the **Imperial Hotel**. Pop inside to see the sole remains of Frank Lloyd Wright's original design in the hotel's **Old Imperial Bar** ⓫ *(see p.121)*, tucked away on the mezzanine floor of the main building. For something more rustic, head back towards Yurakucho Station, where under the railway tracks is the atmospheric tavern **Shin-hinomoto**, see ⓘ④.

Local History
Originally where the Tokugawa silver guild *(gin-za)* and mint were relocated in 1612, Ginza took on a new lease of life after a fire destroyed most of its buildings in 1872. English architect Josiah Conder was hired to design a Western-style shopping boulevard which, when completed, boasted hundreds of red-brick buildings, tiled pavements, a horse-trolley and the city's first gas lamps.

Kabuki on the Move
From April 2010, Kabuki-za is due for demolition and redevelopment into a modern office-theatre complex. During the three-year construction period *kabuki* will be performed at Shimbashi's Embujo Theatre *(see p.22)*.

BRIDGESTONE MUSEUM OF ART

ROPPONGI & AKASAKA

Once notorious nightlife districts, both Roppongi and Akasaka have become places to explore during the day for their art galleries and design delights, as well as great shopping and dining opportunities.

DISTANCE 8km (5 miles)
TIME A leisurely day
START Roppongi Station
END Akasaka Station
POINTS TO NOTE
Don't do this walk on Tuesday if you want to visit the art galleries on the route.

Art Triangle Roppongi

The National Art Centre, Suntory Museum of Art and Mori Art Museum form the three corners of the project Art Triangle Roppongi. Keep your ticket stub after visiting any of these three museums and it will entitle you to reduced entry at each of the others. A map showing other galleries in the area is also available at each museum or online at www.mori.art.museum/eng/atro/index.html.

Food and Drink
① BOTANICA

4F Garden Terrace, Tokyo Midtown, 9-7-4 Akasaka, Minato-ku; tel: 5413 3282; www.conran-restaurants.jp; Mon–Fri 11am–10.30pm, Sat–Sun 11am–9pm; station: Roppongi; ¥¥¥
Enjoy garden views from the terrace of this stylishly British restaurant, part of Sir Terence Conran's portfolio, either over lunch or afternoon tea. A cheaper alternative is Midtown's basement food court, Okawari.jp.

To the southwest of the Imperial Palace, the area of Roppongi, meaning 'six trees', was once a garrison town for the Meiji government. After World War II the American occupation forces established barracks here, giving it its start as the hub of Tokyo's international nightlife. Once infamous for its pick-up bars, the area is undergoing a cultural makeover to become a focus for the city's contemporary art and design scenes, following the success of the upscale Roppongi Hills and Tokyo Midtown complexes, which combine luxury shopping, hotels and restaurants with offices and galleries.

Down the hill, nearby Akasaka is as busy with office workers and politicians by day as it is with restaurant- and bar-goers by night. It's also home to one of the city's most important shrines, as well as the TBS Broadcasting Centre.

ROPPONGI

Emerging from Roppongi Station at exit 4, find your bearings at **Roppongi Crossing** ① (Roppongi kosaten). On the other side of the road, under the raised expressway, you will see the pink and white stripes of the Almond Coffee Shop, while to your left along Gaien-Higashi-dori is the Hotel Ibis – head in this direction towards the 248m (813ft) Midtown Tower, anchor of the vast Tokyo Midtown development.

Tokyo Midtown

Covering nearly 70,000 sq m (753,470 sq ft), **Tokyo Midtown** ❷ (www.tokyo-midtown.com) is its own elegant world of offices, shops, apartments, a convention centre, two museum-galleries and other public facilities. Behind Midtown Tower you will find the small traditional garden of **Hinokicho Park** (Hinokicho-koen), while throughout the complex are interesting pieces of contemporary sculpture. There's a bewildering array of restaurants and cafés here – for something upmarket try **Botanica**, see 🍴①.

Apart from indulging in some shopping or dining, you may wish to spend some time exploring the complex's two museum-galleries.

The focus is on traditional Japanese arts, such as lacquerware, ceramics and textiles, at the small but classy **Suntory Museum of Art** ❸ (tel: 3470 1073; www.suntory.co.jp/sma; Sun–Mon 10am–6pm, Wed–Sat 10am–8pm; charge), in the northern corner of the complex. The building, designed by Kengo Kuma, also has a traditional tea-ceremony room.

Above from far left: upscale shopping in Tokyo Midtown; Roppongi Hills.

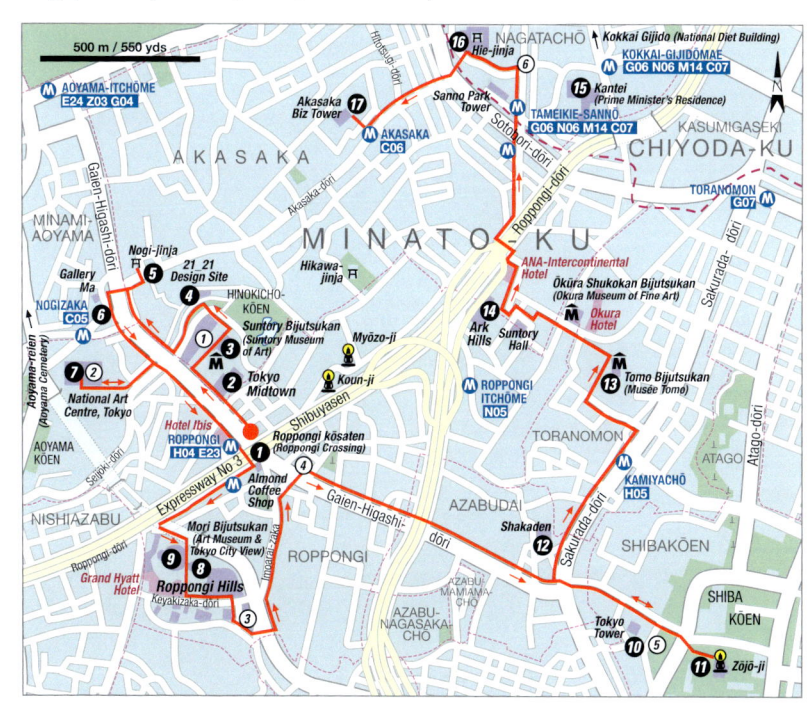

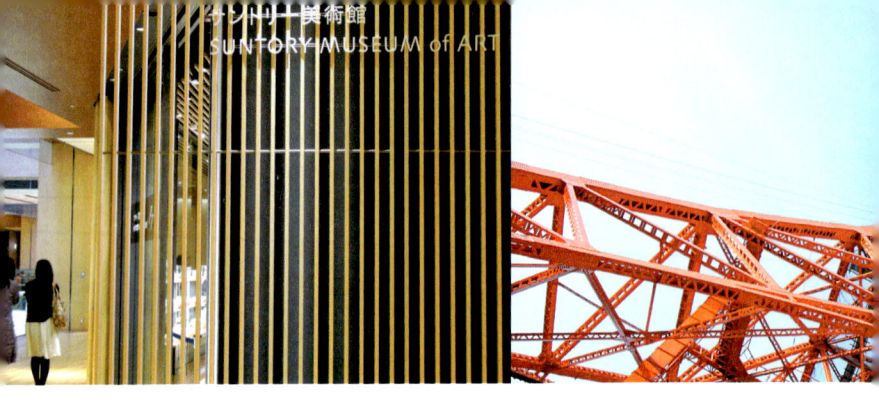

General Nogi

The house in which General Nogi and his wife, following samurai tradition, committed ritual suicide on the death of the emperor Meiji, is within the grounds of the Nogi-jinja. It's open just two days a year (12 and 13 Sept, 9.30am–4.30pm; free).

The angular construction jutting out of the lawn to the rear of Tokyo Midtown is the **21_21 Design Sight** ❹ (tel: 3475 2121; www.2121designsight.jp; daily 11am–8.30pm; charge), the result of a collaboration between architect Ando Tadao and fashion designer Issey Miyake. The main gallery, which is below ground, holds exhibitions on specific themes from a range of designers.

Nogi-jinja

A five-minute walk north of Tokyo Midtown along Gaien-Higashi-dori, across the road from Nogizaka subway station, is **Nogi-jinja** ❺ (tel: 3478 3001; www.nogijinja.or.jp; daily 8.30am–5pm). The shrine is named after General Nogi Maresuke, a hero of the Russo-Japanese War of 1904, who is buried with his wife in nearby Aoyama Cemetery. On the second Sunday of every month an antiques flea market is held in the shrine's grounds.

Gallery Ma

Across the main road, check out what's showing at **Gallery Ma** ❻ (tel: 3402 1010; www.toto.co.jp/gallerma; Tue–Sat 11am–6pm, Fri until 7pm; free), which mounts exhibitions on interior design and architecture from both Japan and overseas; past subjects have included the likes of Ando Tadao. The gallery is on the third floor of a showroom for Toto, Japan's largest toilet manufacturer, so you can also check out the latest in bathroom design while you are here.

National Art Centre, Tokyo

Retrace your steps along Gaien-Higashi-dori back towards Tokyo Midtown, where you should turn right to reach the wavy glass-wall façade of the **National Art Centre, Tokyo** ❼ (NACT; tel: 6812 9900; www.nact.jp; Wed–Mon 10am–6pm; charge). Designed by Kurokawa Kisha, this 48,000-sq m (516,600-sq ft) building is Japan's largest such gallery, staging everything from blockbuster exhibitions of major artists to small-scale shows for local art groups. The atrium foyer is studded with three-storey-tall conical pods – on the top of one you will find **Brasserie Paul Bocuse Le Musée**, see ⑪②. For unusual souvenirs, look in the shop in the National Art Centre's basement.

Roppongi Hills

Return to Roppongi Crossing, turn right and follow Roppongi-dori towards **Roppongi Hills** ❽ (www.roppongihills.com), a complex that is among the brashest of Tokyo's mini-cities. Its 54-storey tower, de-luxe **Grand Hyatt** hotel *(see p.109)*, nine-screen cinema and over 200 shops form one of the largest developments in Japan. In the plaza outside the entrance to the Mori Tower you will see Louise Bourgeois's *Maman*, an iconic sculpture of a giant spider that has become to Roppongi Hills what Hachiko is to Shibuya *(see p.47)*.

The top floors of the **Mori Tower** are occupied by the **Mori Art Museum** ❾ (MAM, Mori Bijutsukan; tel: 5777 8600; www.mori.art.museum; Tue 10am–5pm, Wed–Mon 10am–10pm; charge), hosting exhibitions of mainly contemporary works from Japan and abroad, with a focus on Asian artists. You can combine a visit to the museum with the **Tokyo City View** (daily 9am–11pm; charge) observation deck and, weather permitting, go out on the tower's roof to take in the panorama from the **Sky Deck** (daily 10am–8pm; charge).

Refreshment Options
Return to ground level, exit onto boutique-lined Keyakizaka-dori and take the side road behind the Tsutaya book, CD and DVD store to find the Singaporean restaurant **Hainan Jeefan Shokudo**, see ❸.

Across the road from Tsutaya, turn left then right to follow Imoarai-zaka uphill back towards Roppongi Crossing. Just before reaching there, branch right to emerge on Gaien-Higashi-dori and the heart of Roppongi's main drag of bars and nightclubs. Here you will find **Kina**, see ❹, an old-style café that's worth checking out day or night.

Tokyo Tower
Keep on walking east along Gaien-Higashi-dori, passing under the raised expressway towards the orange-and-white-painted **Tokyo Tower** ❿ (tel: 3433 5111; www.tokyotower.co.jp; daily 9am–10pm; charge). Even though it no longer offers the highest vantage point over the city, it's still worth getting close up to this Tokyo icon to admire its Eiffel Tower-like structure. Amid the gaggle of restaurants and other amusements closer to the ground, you can fuel up at **Tokyo Curry Lab**, see ❺.

Above from far left: Suntory Museum of Art; Tokyo Tower; art atop the Mori Tower in Roppongi Hills.

Food and Drink

② **BRASSERIE PAUL BOCUSE LE MUSÉE**
National Art Centre, 7-22-2 Roppongi, Minato-ku; tel: 5770 8161; www.hiramatsu.co.jp; Wed–Mon 11am–9pm; station: Roppongi; ¥¥¥
Bookings aren't taken, so come early or late if you want to avoid queuing up for lunch at this classy French operation, notable for its location atop one of the giant concrete cones in the Art Centre's lobby.

③ **HAINAN JEEFAN SHOKUDO**
6-11-16 Roppongi, Minato-ku; tel: 5474 3200; Mon–Fri 11.30am–2pm and 6pm–midnight, Sat–Sun 11.30am–3pm and 6–11pm; station: Roppongi; ¥¥
Tasty Singaporean street-food, such as chicken rice and spicy noodles, are served up at this cute place near Roppongi Hills.

④ **KINA**
3-13-12 Roppongi, Minato-ku; tel: 3478 1678; www.kina-roppongi.com; Mon–Fri noon–11pm, Sat noon–9pm; station: Roppongi; ¥
This 1970s *kissaten* (café), with incredibly funky lights and waiters in wine-red jackets and bowties, is retro heaven. There are set menus of Japanese tea and traditional sweets, as well as finger sandwiches, beers and cocktails.

⑤ **TOKYO CURRY LAB**
2F Tokyo Tower, 4-2-8 Shiba-koen, Minato-ku; tel: 5425 2900; daily 11am–9pm; station: Kamiyacho; ¥¥
Tokyo's Tower's dining options are far from chic, but design fans will enjoy the clean lines and concept of this simple eatery celebrating Japan's unique take on curry and rice.

Sanno Matsuri

Every two years in June, Hie-jinja is the stage for the massive Sanno Matsuri festival. Participants in period costumes take part in an impressive parade, which includes the carrying of heavy *mikoshi* (portable shrines) on the shoulders of locals.

Zojo-ji

Adjacent to Tokyo Tower in **Shiba Park** (Shiba-koen) sits one of Tokyo's most impressive temples – **Zoju-ji** ⓫ (tel: 3432 1413; www.zozoji.or.jp; daily 6am–5.30pm). Founded in 1393, the site was chosen by the Tokugawa clan in the late 1600s as their ancestral temple; six of the Tokugawa shoguns are buried here. Close to the bay and the Tokaido (East Sea Road), it also served as a post station for travellers. Most of the temple buildings, once numbering over 100, have not survived the ravages of time, but its main entrance, the 1612 red-lacquered San-mon, is original. The Main Hall (Taiden) contains ancient sutras and statuary.

Shakaden

Return to Tokyo Tower and turn right on Sakurada-dori to walk towards Kamiyacho subway station, passing the striking **Shakaden** ⓬. With its enormous, wedge-like black roof it may look like an alien spaceship, but this is the Tokyo headquarters of the Reiyukai Buddhist movement (www.reiyukai india.org/shakaden.asp).

Musée Tomo

Walk past the entrances to Kamiyacho Station and turn left, heading uphill towards the Toranomon Tower complex. Walk through this towards the **Okura Hotel** *(see p.109)* to encounter the **Musée Tomo** ⓭ (Tomo Bijutsukan; 4-1-35 Toranomon, Minato-ku; tel: 5733 5131; www.musee-tomo.or.jp; Tue–Sun 11am–6pm; charge), a small but highly elegant museum housing the contemporary Japanese ceramics collection of Tomo Kikuchi.

Ark Hills

Head west from the Okura Hotel to arrive at the rear of the **Ark Hills** ⓮ complex, a precursor of Roppongi Hills. Located here is the ANA Interconti-

Food and Drink

⑥ KUROSAWA

2-7-9 Nagatacho, Chiyoda-ku; tel: 3580 9638; Mon–Fri 11.30am–3pm and 5–10pm, Sat noon–9pm; station: Tameike-sanno; ¥¥

Enjoy gourmet *soba* noodle-and-pork dishes in this atmospheric restaurant that takes its design cues from Akira Kurosawa's movies.

High-Rise Tokyo

At 333m (1,092ft) tall, Tokyo Tower, built in 1958, is one of the city's tallest structures, even if its top-most observation deck only lets you go up to 250m (820ft). The Mori Tower in Roppongi Hills allows visitors access to its rooftop observation deck at 270m (885ft), while nearby you can sip cocktails and look out of the 248m (7,375ft) tall Midtown Tower from the lobby of the Ritz-Carlton Hotel. There are also not-quite-so-lofty observation decks in several of the skyscrapers that cluster in Shinjuku, including the Tokyo Metropolitan Government Building *(see p.50)*. As of 2011, however, all these will be dwarfed by the 610m (8,560ft) Tokyo Sky Tree (www.tokyo-skytree.jp) in the Narihirabashi/Oshiage area, east across the Sumida River from Asakusa; the building's topmost observation point will be at the giddy height of 450m (1,475ft).

nental Hotel and the classical-music venue **Suntory Hall** (tel: 3505 1001; www.suntory.com/culture-sports/suntoryhall). You will emerge back on Roppongi-dori facing the raised expressway.

AKASAKA

Kantei

Cross Roppongi-dori to enter Akasaka. Walk towards Tameike-Sanno subway station, near to which you can see the Sanno Park Tower and the handsome residence of Japan's prime minister, known as the **Kantei** ⓯. You can't go inside, but you can take a virtual tour (see www.kantei.go.jp/foreign/vt/index.html). A short distance to the north, Japan's parliament sits in the **National Diet Building** (Kokkai Gijido).

Hie-jinja

Next to Sanno Park Tower, steps lead up to one of Tokyo's premier shrines – **Hie-jinja** ⓰ (tel: 3581 2471; www.hiejinja.net; daily Apr–Sept 5am–6pm, Oct–Mar 6am–5pm). Transplanted to the borders of the Akasaka and Nagatacho districts in the 17th century in the belief that it would help to deflect evil from Edo Castle, the shrine's current buildings were erected in 1967. Its role as protector is still evident today; look carefully at a carving to the left of the main shrine and you will see a monkey cradling its baby. Pregnant women come here to pay homage to the image. Downhill from the shrine, away from the main road, you will find the restaurant **Kurosawa**, see ⑪⑥.

Akasaka Biz Tower

Leave the shrine the way you entered, cross the street and head southwest for a couple of blocks to reach the **Akasaka Biz Tower** ⓱ (www.akasakabiztower.com), another of the area's new dining, shopping and business complexes. Nearby is Akasaka Station.

Above: statues of the bodhisattva Jizo at Zojo-ji – each is for the soul of a departed child.

Below: Mori Tower.

AOYAMA & HARAJUKU

These two western quarters are known for their high-fashion boutiques. But you can also find traditional and contemporary art galleries and the city's top Shinto shrine, hidden in a forest that also harbours a beautiful iris garden.

DISTANCE 5.5km (3½ miles)
TIME 6 hours
START Omotesando Station
END Kita-Sando or Harajuku stations
POINTS TO NOTE
Almost all the area's boutiques are open from 11am or noon to 8pm, so it's best to start this walk late morning or early afternoon. To see some outrageous costumes, come on a Sunday when *cosplayers* (fans dressed as their favourite *anime* characters or pop idols) hang out around Harajuku Station.

Below: La Collezione.

Once a post station on the Kamakura Kaido, a road that ran from the 11th-century imperial capital of Kamakura *(see p.84)* to the remote northern reaches, Harajuku is now associated with all that is trendy, from streetwear to designer labels such as Louis Vuitton and Dior, branches of which are clustered along super-stylish Omotesando. At this zelkova tree-lined boulevard's eastern end is the high-fashion district of Aoyama. Here you can view some great examples of modern architecture.

AOYAMA

From exit A4 of Omotesando Station emerge at the narrow end of Omotesando near the boutiques of some of Japan's top fashion talent, such as **Issey Miyake** (3-18-11 Minami-Aoyama, Minato-ku; tel: 3423 1407; www.isseymiyake.co.jp), **Yoji Yamamoto** (5-3-6 Minami-Aoyama; tel: 3409 6006; www.yohjiyamamoto.co.jp) and Kawakubo Rei, designer for **Comme des Garçons** (5-2-1 Minami-Aoyama; tel: 3406 3951). The most striking boutique is **Prada** ❶ (5-2-6 Minami-Aoyama; tel: 6418 0400), in a giant bubble-wrapped glass structure designed by architects Jacques Herzog and Pierre de Meuron.

Japanese design strikes back towards the end of the street at **La Collezione** ❷, a work by Pritzker Prize-winning architect Ando Tadao, where shops and offices are housed within a cylinder of concrete. You will see one of Ando's more recent projects later on this walk.

Nezu Museum of Art

At the end of Omotesando is the **Nezu Museum of Art** ❸ (Nezu Bijutsukan; Tue–Sun 9.30am–4.30pm; charge), with its ceramics, textiles, calligraphy, paintings and tea-ceremony utensils. Among its treasures are the Kamakura-period Nanchi Waterfall scroll painting and Ogata Korin's *Irises* (only displayed in the last week of April and early May). The museum's sloping garden, with its pond, teahouse and stupas, is a gem.

Return to the main Omotesando crossing, perhaps pausing for refreshments at the elegant café and confectioner's **Yoku Moku**, see ①.

Food and Drink
① **YOKU MOKU**
5-3-3 Minami-Aoyama, Minato-ku; tel: 5485 3330; daily 10am–7pm; station: Omotesando; ¥
Famous for its crisp, wafer-thin rolled biscuits, this blue-tiled café is an elegant place for refreshments, of which you partake in an outdoor courtyard.

Above from far left: Prada's distinctive shopfront; Jingu Naien, Meiji-jingu's iris garden.

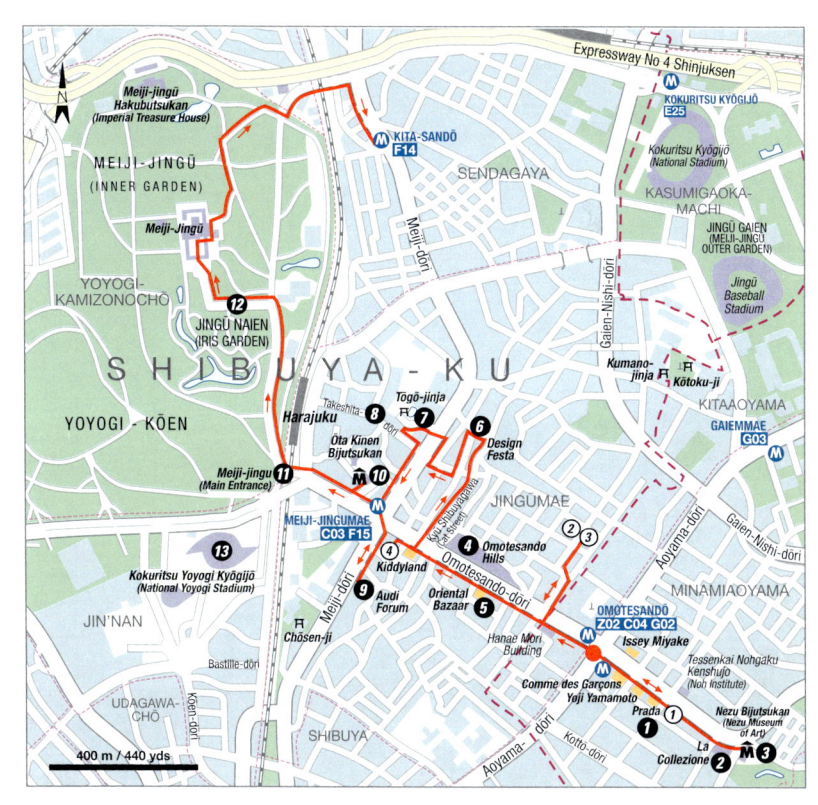

NEZU MUSEUM OF ART 43

Above from left: barrels of sake brought for blessing at Meiji-jingu; Kiddyland kitsch.

HARAJUKU

Walk northwest along Omotesando, heading into Harajuku; halfway down the boulevard's main section, on the right-hand side, you will find Ando Tadao's second contribution – **Omotesando Hills** ❹ (www.omotesandohills.com). This complex of shops and apartments deliberately stays beneath the treeline outside, while inside it burrows deep into the ground to create a striking central atrium encircled by a spiralling walkway that replicates the angle and incline of the pavement. There are several places to eat and drink here, but also worth searching out on the backstreets to the northeast are the venerable *tonkatsu* restaurant **Maisen**, see ②, or the trendy café-bar **unmarble**, see ③.

Across the road, you can't miss the mock-traditional architecture of the red-and-green-painted **Oriental Bazaar** ❺ (5-9-13 Jingumae, Shibuya-ku; tel: 3400 3933; www.orientalbazaar.co.jp), a large gift shop targeted at the foreign buyer. On the upper floors you will find a decent selection of genuine antiques.

Nearby is **Kiddyland** (6-1-9 Jingumae, Shibuya-ku; tel: 3409 3431; www.kiddyland.co.jp), one of the city's best toy stores, and the funky restaurant **Fujimamas**, see ④.

Design Festa

Across the road from Kiddyland is **Cat Street**, packed with emerging boutiques that provide a youthful counterpoint to the adult sophistication of Omotesando. Stroll north along it until you reach the entrance to **Design Festa** ❻ (tel: 3479 1442; www.designfesta.com; daily 11am–8pm; free), a colourful explosion of contemporary-art galleries based in several old houses and an apartment block.

Togo-jinja

Work your way west towards Meiji-dori and the main entrance to the shrine **Togo-jinja** ❼. Admiral Togo Heihachiro's ships vanquished the Russian fleet in the Tsushima Straits in the 1904–5 Russo-Japanese War. An excellent antiques and flea market is held in the grounds of the shrine on the first and fourth Sunday of the month from 8am to around 2pm.

Food and Drink

② MAISEN
4-8-5 Jingumae, Shibuya-ku; tel: 3470 0071; daily 11am–10pm; station: Omotesando; ¥¥
This well-regarded *tonkatsu* (deep-fried breaded pork cutlets) restaurant, based in a former bathhouse, also serves deep-fried chicken and oysters. English menu available.

③ UNMARBLE
4-5-12 Jingumae, Shibuya-ku; tel: 5474 3373; www.unmarble.jp; daily 11.30am–midnight; station: Omotesando; ¥
Hipster bar and café with a laid-back vibe, contemporary furnishing and decent set lunch menus for under ¥1,000.

④ FUJIMAMAS
6-3-2 Jingumae, Shibuya-ku; tel: 5485 2262; www.fujimamas.com; daily 11am–11pm; station: Meiji-jingumae; ¥¥¥
American-Asian cuisine with a few Latin flavours in a spacious wood-frame house – Tokyo at its most hip and eclectic.

Takeshita-dori

Exit Togo-jinja's grounds directly into the consumer mayhem of **Takeshita-dori** ❽, a narrow pedestrian street packed with cheap fashion, jewellery and knick-knack stores that are constantly thronged with teenagers; at weekends this may well be the most densely crowded place in the city. A right turn leads you to the Takeshita entrance of Harajuku Station, while a left turn brings you back to the relative calm of Meiji-dori.

Audi Forum

Continue south along Meiji-dori crossing Omotesando until you hit, on the left, the **Audi Forum** ❾ (www.audi.co.jp), one of the area's most extraordinary new buildings. Designed by British architect Benjamin Warner, this multi-faceted glass building looks like a giant crystal shard.

Ota Memorial Museum of Art

Return to Omotesando, turn left uphill and take the first lane on the right when you see a branch of the home-goods store Muji to find the excellent **Ota Memorial Museum of Art** ❿ (Ota Kinen Bijutsukan; 1-10-10 Jingumae, Shibuya-ku; tel: 3403 0880; www.ukiyoe-ota-muse.jp; Tue–Sun 10.30am–5pm; charge). The galleries feature monthly selections from a body of more than 12,000 *ukiyo-e* woodblock prints, many by masters of the genre like Hiroshige, Utamaru and Hokusai.

Meiji-jingu

Return to Omotesando and head uphill to reach the main mock-Tudor entrance to Harajuku Station, built in 1924. Cross the bridge over the tracks and bear right. A huge cypress *torii* gate announces the main entrance to **Meiji-jingu** ⓫ (tel: 3379 5511; www.meijijingu.or.jp), Tokyo's premier Shinto shrine, deifying the memory of the emperor Meiji, who died in 1912. This is the Inner Garden; the Outer Garden is around 1km (²⁄₃ mile) to the east and contains several sports stadia. The main shrine buildings are about 1km (²⁄₃ mile) from the entrance along a broad gravel path through a forest.

On the left, just before you turn into Meiji-jingu's central complex, is the entrance to the **Jingu Naien** ⓬ (daily 8.30am–5pm; charge). In June crowds flock to this lush garden, with an old teahouse overlooking a lily pond, to see around 100 different species of iris bloom; at other times of the year may just have the place to yourself.

Yoyogi Park

If you leave by the northern gate, the nearest subway station is Kita-Sando on Meiji-dori. Otherwise return to the Harajuku exit and, if you desire more open space, pop into the neighbouring **Yoyogi Park** (Yoyogi-koen). Also take a moment to admire the fluid lines of concrete tents and pavilions that make up Kenzo Tange's **National Yoyogi Stadium** ⓭, opposite Harajuku Station.

A Classic Shrine

The original Meiji-jingu burnt down in an air raid in 1945, but the present buildings, erected in 1958, are a faithful reconstruction. The beautifully understated Shinto design is distinguished by its cypress pillars, sloping copper roofs and immaculate white gravel forecourt. Over 4 million people visit during the first four days of New Year to pay their respects, and throughout the year there are several other festivals celebrated at the shrine, some including ceremonial archery and *bugaku* – court music and dances.

Yoyogi's History

This was once a military training ground requisitioned by the US occupation forces after the war and used to house military personnel. The land was handed back in 1964 to become a village for athletes attending the Tokyo Olympic Games.

SHIBUYA & EBISU

This walk through the teen-trend Mecca of Shibuya and neighbouring district of Ebisu has something for everyone, including the kids and lovers of quirky museums and contemporary art.

DISTANCE 4km (2½ miles)
TIME 4–6 hours
START Shibuya Station
END Ebisu Station
POINTS TO NOTE

This walk can be combined with Aoyama and Harajuku (walk 4) by catching the train or subway to Shibuya or walking about 10 minutes between the two areas. Do it towards the late afternoon to see Shibuya in its neon-lit brilliance.

As late as the 1880s, tea plantations covered the slopes that surround the valley known as Shibuya, and even by the turn of the 19th century it was still very much Tokyo's rural edge. As with Shinjuku and Ikebukuro, the coming of the railways, and the department stores attached to them, changed all that. Today, this vibrant entertainment and shopping district is one of the most exciting in Tokyo, the centre from which fashion trends ripple out to the rest of Japan. This walk also takes you to the neighbouring area of Ebisu, named after a Shinto god of good fortune and the site of a one-time brewery now morphed into a complex of shops, restaurants and cultural facilities.

SHIBUYA

Several train and subway lines converge on Shibuya Station. From wherever you arrive, make your way through the Tokyu Toyoko department store towards the western side, which houses the terminus for the Keio-Inokashira line (you can hop on this later to visit the Japan Folk Crafts Museum, *see feature, right*). On the way you will pass a giant 14-panel painting, *Myth of*

Tomorrow ❶ *(Asu no Shinwa)* by Okamoto Taro (1911–96), a powerful *Guernica*-like mural of the atomic-bomb explosion. Originally created in the late 1960s for a luxury hotel in Mexico, the monumental work was rediscovered in 2003 and took five years to be restored and find its new home in the station.

Hachiko Statue

Out of the window facing the Okamoto mural you will have a good view over **Shibuya Crossing** (Shibuya kosaten), a mesmerising confluence of neon, giant video screens and endless streams of people. Emerge at ground level in the plaza outside the station and dig among the crowds to find the statue of the faithful dog **Hachiko** ❷, one of Tokyo's most famous meeting spots *(see margin, right)*.

Tepco Electric Energy Museum

Take the road heading immediately north of the plaza past department stores Seibu (on the left) and Marui (on both sides) towards **Tower Records** (tel: 3496 3661; www.towerrecords.co.jp; daily 10am–10pm), one of the largest and best places to buy CDs, DVDs and books. A block further north, on the left, is the **Tepco Electric Energy Museum** ❸ (Denryokukan; 1-12-10 Jinnan, Shibuya-ku; tel: 3477 1191; www.denryokukan.com; Thur–Tue 10am–6pm; charge). The eight-storey museum, run by the Tokyo Electric Power Company (Tepco), has interactive displays on every aspect of electricity. It's very popular with kids.

Tobacco and Salt Museum

After the museum, take the next turning left and walk uphill to Koen-dori, emerging opposite Shibuya Ward Office. Turn left and walk downhill to the quirky **Tobacco and Salt Museum** ❹ (Tabako to Shio no Hakubutsukan; 1-16-8 Jinnan, Shibuya-ku; tel: 3476 2041; www.jti.co.jp; Tue–Sun 10am–5.30pm; charge). Salt and tobacco were a government monopoly until the early 20th century, and remained under strict state control until 1985. The museum traces the history of salt and tobacco production in Japan and overseas through displays that include smoking implements and salt sculptures. The highlight is the fourth-floor special exhibition of *ukiyo-e* woodblock prints of courtesans and other Edo-period figures relaxing as they prepare their pipes.

Above from far left: Shibuya Crossing; old Japanese cigarette boxes at the Tobacco and Salt Museum.

Faithful Friend
An Akita breed, Hachiko belonged to a Tokyo University professor who lived in Shibuya in the 1920s. The dog accompanied him to the station each morning, and met him there promptly every evening. When the professor died in 1925, Hachiko continued turning up at the station for the next decade until her own death, earning the affection of locals for exemplifying loyalty to a master.

Japan Folk Crafts Museum

The outstanding Japan Folk Crafts Museum (Mingei-kan; 4-3-33 Komaba, Meguro-ku; tel: 3467 4527; www.mingeikan.or.jp; Tue–Sun 10am–5pm; charge) is located two stops from Shibuya on the Keio-Inokashira line. Alight at Komaba-Todaimae Station and walk northwest for a couple of minutes to find the lovely old building constructed of wood and stone, and once owned by master potter Yanagi Soetsu. A variety of ceramics, furniture and textiles are exhibited in this shrine to *mingei*, Japan's folk-craft movement.

Dogenzaka

This street is named after the highway robber Dogen who once waylaid travellers on this slope (*zaka*). Walking away from Shibuya Station up Dogenzaka, to the right you will find an area dense with love hotels – the rent-by-the-hour places patronised by Tokyo couples looking for a little privacy.

Below: 109 Building.

Tokyo Wonder Site

One block south, take a break for refreshments at **Kurage**, see ⑪①. In the same building is a gallery that's part of the **Tokyo Wonder Site** ❺ (tel: 3463 0603; www.tokyo-ws.org; Tue–Sun 11am–7pm; free). Always worth a look inside, the project is dedicated to the generation and promotion of contemporary art and culture in Tokyo.

Tokyu Hands

Cross Koen-dori and walk between the fashion stores **Parco Part II** and **Parco Part I** towards **Tokyu Hands** ❻ (tel: 5489 5111; www.tokyu-hands.co.jp; daily 10am–8pm, closed 2nd and 3rd Wed of month) on the left. This home-improvements and hobbies store is a great place for souvenirs, creative materials and outdoor goods of all kinds.

Bunkamura

Head southwest towards Bunkamura-dori to find the main Tokyu department store and the attached arts centre **Bunkamura** ❼ (tel: 3477 9111; www.bunkamura.co.jp). Meaning 'culture village', the complex offers art galleries, a cinema, a theatre and the 2,150-seat **Orchard Hall**, an acoustically excellent shoebox-style hall used for classical-music concerts. Also here is **Les Deux Magots**, see ⑪②.

109 Building

Running parallel to the north of Bunkamura-dori is narrow Centre Gai, a pedestrian street that acts as a catwalk of the latest Shibuya fashion. Having picked out some ideas, proceed to the distinctive silver silo of the **109 Building** ❽ (2-29-1 Dogenzaka, Shibuya-ku; tel: 3477 5111; www.shibuya109.jp; daily 10am–9pm) at the apex of Bunkamori-dori and Dogenzaka *(see margin, left)*. This Shibuya landmark embodies the trends and culture of the teenage girls who play a leading role in Japanese consumer culture. Even if you don't fit into the targeted demographic, just walking through the countless boutiques filled with young fashionistas and echoing with dance music is quite an adventure.

YEBISU GARDEN PLACE

Walk east to return to Shibuya Station and take the JR Yamanote line one stop south to **Ebisu**. A moving walkway links the station with **Yebisu Garden Place** ❾ (www.gardenplace.jp), built on the site of the old Sapporo brewery. The spacious complex includes shops, restaurants, the Westin Hotel, a 39-storey tower, a cinema, a performance hall and a mock-French chateau housing a Joël Robuchon restaurant.

Two Museums

Learn about the brewery that used to be here at the **Yebisu Beer Museum** ❿ (tel: 5423 7255; www.sapporobeer.jp; Tue–Sun 10am–6pm; free), which includes a virtual-reality tour that explains aspects of the brewing process and an opportunity to sample some of Sapporo's beers (charge).

On the complex's eastern side is the superb **Tokyo Metropolitan Photography Museum** ⓫ (Tokyo-to Shashin Bijutsukan; tel: 3280 0031; www.syabi.com; Tue–Sun 10am–6pm, Thur–Fri until 8pm; charge), the city's premier exhibition space for notable photography and video art.

Before leaving Yebisu Garden Place you could grab something to eat at **Chibo**, see ③, on the 38th floor of the tower. Alternatively, return to Ebisu Station, just northwest of which you will find delicious grilled chicken and sake at **Ebisu Imaiya**, see ④.

Above from far left: two snapshots of Yebisu Garden Place.

Food and Drink

① KURAGE
1-19-8 Jin'nan, Shibuya-ku; tel: 3463-3323; daily 10am–11.30pm; station: Shibuya; ¥
The ground floor of the Shibuya Workers' Welfare Hall houses this trendy café, offering a great-value deli lunch plus internet access.

② LES DEUX MAGOTS
2-24-1 Dogenzaka, Shibuya-ku; tel: 3477 9124; www.bunkamura.co.jp; daily 11am–10.30pm; station: Shibuya; ¥
Wind down over a cup of coffee or a glass of wine at this branch of the famous Parisian café-bistro inside the Bunkamura arts complex.

③ CHIBO
38F Yebisu Garden Place Tower, 4-20-3 Ebisu, Shibuya-ku; tel: 5424 1011; Mon–Fri 11.30am–2.30pm and 5–10pm, Sat–Sun 11.30am–10pm; station: Ebisu; ¥¥
Okonomiyaki (savoury pancakes) are made before your eyes on grills set in the table. Fun food and never expensive, plus a brilliant view.

④ EBISU IMAIYA
1-7-11 Ebisu-Nishi, Shibuya-ku; tel: 5456 0255; Sat–Thur 5pm–2am, Fri 5pm–4am; station: Ebisu; ¥¥
Delectable free-range chicken, served either as *yakitori* (charcoal-grilled) or in warming hotpots. Spotless and efficient, and everything is explained in English.

SHINJUKU

Split by Japan's busiest station, one side of Shinjuku is dominated by sky-high architecture, the other by shops and a neon-festooned entertainment area – a sometimes seedy, but enthralling legacy of Tokyo's old pleasure districts.

DISTANCE 8km (5 miles)
TIME A leisurely day
START Tochomae Station
END Shinjuku Station
POINTS TO NOTE
Save yourself the hassle of working out which of the hundreds of exits from Shinjuku Station to take by alighting instead at Tochomae, the subway stop closest to the Tokyo Metropolitan Government Office. Note the early closing time of Shinjuku Garden (last entry at 4pm).

Visitor Information

The best place for information about the city is the Tokyo Tourist Information Centre (1F Tokyo Metropolitan Government No. 1 Building, 2-8-1 Nishi-Shinjuku, Shinjuku-ku; tel: 5321 3077; www.tourism. metro.tokyo.jp; daily 9.30am–6.30pm). Come here to find out about 10 free guided tours of the city.

A microcosm of Tokyo, Shinjuku offers soaring high-rises, massive malls, tiny shops, classy boutiques, a beautiful and spacious garden and a maze of entertainment venues. The district is home to infamous Kabukicho, Japan's largest red-light district, but just a short stroll away is the imposing Tokyo Metropolitan Government Office. The area is a fertile ground for shopping, dining, people-watching and simply taking in all that is contemporary Japan.

A thick band of railway lines splits the district, west of the centre, into Nishi (West) and Higashi (East) Shinjuku.

WEST SHINJUKU

If you haven't emerged from Tochomae Station in West Shinjuku, then orientate yourself towards the western exit of Shinjuku Station and the fountains at the centre of the sunken plaza just in front of Odakyu department store. An underground walkway beneath Chuodori runs from here to the first sight.

Tokyo Metropolitan Government Office

Designed by award-winning architect Kenzo Tange, the **Tokyo Metropolitan Government Office** ❶ (also known as the **Tocho**) is the city's governmental nerve centre. Its monumental yet elegant design, with twin 48-storey towers, makes it stand out amid a grove of fellow skyscrapers at the end of Chuo-dori.

Head up to the 45th floor of either tower to take in the panoramic view from the **Observation Rooms** (tel: 5320 7890; www.metro.tokyo.jp; Mon–Fri 9.30am–10pm, Sat–Sun 9.30am–7pm; free). On a clear day you will be rewarded with a panorama that stretches from Mount Fuji to the hills of the Boso Peninsula in Chiba Prefecture. You can also take a 40-minute tour of the complex (Mon–Fri 10am–3pm; free), departing from the **Tokyo Tourist Information Centre** *(see margin, left)* on the ground floor. Cross over to the scrappy **Shinjuku Chuo Park** (Shinjuku Chuo-koen), from where you can get a good view of the Tocho's exterior design.

Shinjuku Park Tower

Immediately south of the park stands another Tange building, the Postmodernist, 52-storey **Shinjuku Park Tower** ❷. The three stylish linked towers, with their luminous glass pyramids, house the luxurious Park Hyatt Hotel *(see p.111)* and its glamorous **New York Grill** restaurant, see 🍴①. Also here are a number of floors devoted to interior design and architecture, including the first-rate **Living Design Centre Ozae** (tel: 5322 6500; www.ozone.co.jp; Thur–Tue 10.30am–7pm; charge), which has exhibitions relating to modern interior design.

Above from far left: neon Kabukicho; Shinjuku street scene; Tokyo Metropolitan Government Office.

Food and Drink
① NEW YORK GRILL

52F Park Hyatt Hotel, 3-7-1-2 Nishi-Shinjuku, Shinjuku-ku; tel: 5322 1234; daily 11.30am–2.30pm, 5.30–10.30pm; station: Tochomae; ¥¥¥¥

Dine in a sky-view setting at Shinjuku's Park Hyatt Hotel (the setting for the film *Lost in Translation*). Sunday brunch with cocktails at the adjacent New York Bar is an institution for the expat community.

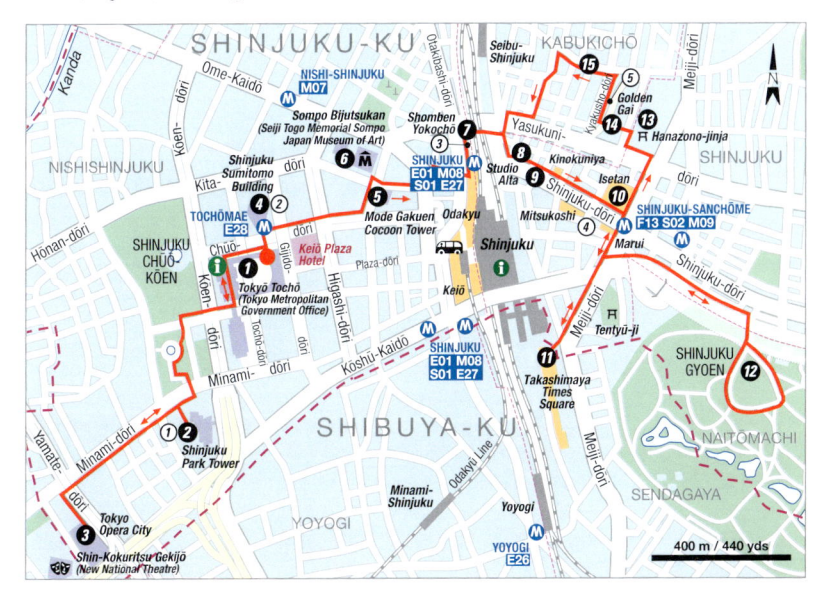

TOKYO METROPOLITAN GOVERNMENT OFFICE 51

Super Station

Seven railway lines and three subways feed over 3.5 million passengers through Shinjuku Station every day, making it the busiest such terminus in the world.

Tokyo Opera City

It's a 10-minute stroll west of the tower along Minami-dori to **Tokyo Opera City** ❸ (www.operacity.jp), a 54-floor complex of shops, offices and restaurants. There's an **art gallery** (tel: 5353 0756; Tue–Sun 11am–7pm; charge) and a **concert hall** (tel: 5353 9999) here, but you are likely to find the most interesting part of the complex to be the **NTT Intercommunication Centre** (tel: 0120-144 199; www.ntticc.or.jp; Tue–Sun 10am–6pm; free), an interactive, high-tech exhibition space, with an electronic library and internet café. Also part of the complex is the **New National Theatre** (tel: 5351 3011; www.nntt.jac.go.jp), housing opera, theatre and modern-dance venues.

Sumitomo Building

Return the way you came to Chuo-dori. Opposite the Tocho is the **Sumitomo Building** ❹. This six-sided construction's atrium stretches from the fourth to the 52nd floor. In case you didn't make it up the Tocho (or just want another bird's-eye view), there's also a free observatory here on the 51st floor, while on the 50th floor you will find **Kuu**, see ⑪②, an excellent lunch spot or place to return to for dinner.

Mode Gakuen Cocoon Tower

Walk east along Chuo-dori towards the ultra-contemporary, cross-hatched **Mode Gakuen Cocoon Tower** ❺, one of the most striking new additions to the Shinjuku skyline. Designed by Tange Associates, and occupied by a

New Lodgings

Shinjuku came into existence because of its position at the junction of two key arteries leading into the city from the west. Shinjuku means 'new lodgings', a reference to a post station built on Koshu Kaido for horses and travellers on their way to Edo in the early 18th century.

Trains first rolled into Shinjuku in 1885. The major factor in its rise, however, was its narrow escape from the 1923 Great Kanto Earthquake. Huge numbers of residents moved in, followed by department stores, theatres and artists' studios. The area's importance made it a target for American bombing, which levelled the entire district on 25 May 1945. Yet by the 1970s it had rebounded with West Shinjuku sprouting a gaggle of skyscrapers (such as the Mode Gakuen Cocoon Tower, *pictured*) that, in a generally low-rise city, still remain striking.

fashion and computer-studies school, this 50-storey glass stunner has a large bookstore, **Book 1st** (www.book1st.net), in its basement; the store includes Tokyo Magazine Centre, stocking some 5,000 titles from around the world.

Seiji Togo Memorial Sompo Japan Museum of Art

One final skyscraper to check out is the Sompo Japan Building behind Mode Gakuen Cocoon Tower on Kita-dori; on the 42nd floor is the **Seiji Togo Memorial Sompo Japan Museum of Art** ❻ (tel: 3349 3080; www.sompo-japan.co.jp; Tue–Sun 10am–5.30pm; charge). Apart from an collection of stylised works by painter Togo Seiji (1897–1978), you can also view one of Vincent van Gogh's *Sunflowers* and other Impressionist paintings by Cézanne and Gauguin.

Shomben Yokocho

Head east to Shinjuku Station, passing between the bus terminal and the Odakyu Halc Building, and crossing over the road to discover a cluttered, run-down four-block neighbourhood called **Shomben Yokocho** ❼ ('Piss Alley'), hung with red lanterns and packed with friendly hole-in-the-wall restaurants and bars. It's a great place to return to in the evening for inexpensive *yakitori* (grilled chicken) and beers. On the southwestern corner of the district you will find the appealing **Tajimaya Coffee House**, see ⑪③.

EAST SHINJUKU

Take a right out of the café and pass a row of discount clothes shops to find a pedestrian tunnel running under the tracks that slice Shinjuku down the middle. You will emerge on the eastern side of the station beside the plaza fronting **Studio Alta** ❽, marked by a giant external video screen – there's always a crowd here, as this is one of the area's most popular meeting spots.

Shinjuku-dori

Turn away from the station and walk along **Shinjuku-dori** ❾, the district's premier shopping street. On the left you will find the original flagship of **Kinokuniya**, one of the city's best bookshops, with a good selection of

Above from far left: Sumitomo Building atrium; Shinjuku-dori.

Food and Drink

② KUU
50F Shinjuku Sumitomo Building, 2-6-1 Nishi-Shinjuku, Shinjuku-ku; tel: 3344 6457; daily noon–2pm, 5–11pm; station: Tochomae; ¥¥

This casual *izakaya* (tavern) in the Sumitomo Building affords panoramic city views. The core of the menu is charcoal-grilled seafood, chicken and seasonal vegetables. This is also an affordable place to explore some different types of premium sake.

③ TAJIMAYA COFFEE HOUSE
Shomben Yokocho, Shinjuku-eki Nishi-guchi, Shinjuku-ku; tel: 3342 0881; www.shinjuku.or.jp/tajimaya; daily 10am–10.30pm; station: Shinjuku; ¥;

Retreat from the crowds swarming through Shinjuku Station at this warm, wood-furnished establishment on the corner of the first set of alleys here. The café serves a first-rate brew and nice cakes.

Above from left:
Kabukicho; Shinjuku National Garden.

English titles; on the right are the department stores Mitsukoshi and Marui. Take the road between these two stores to find the esteemed tempura restaurant **Tsunahachi**, see ①④.

Occupying a block on the corner of Meiji-dori and Shinjuku-dori is the department store **Isetan** ❿ (tel: 3352 1111; www.isetan.co.jp; daily 10am–8pm), Shinjuku's only major building to have survived from the pre-war period. This chic seven-floor emporium has a connected eight-floor Men's Building to the rear, a fabulous basement food hall, a floor devoted to restaurants and a rooftop garden.

Takashimaya Times Square
Follow Meiji-dori south, crossing Koshu Kaido to reach one of Shinjuku's more modern shopping complexes, **Takashimaya Times Square** ⓫, next to the Shin-Minami entrance to Shinjuku Station. As well as a branch of the eponymous Takashimaya store, you will find **Tokyu Hands**, an innovative handicrafts and interior-design store, and the main branch of the bookstore **Kinokuniya**.

Shinjuku National Garden
East Shinjuku is not all about shopping. From Takashimaya Times Square, return to the crossroads of Koshu Kaido and Meiji-dori, and turn right to reach the main entrance of **Shinjuku National Garden** ⓬ (Shinjuku Gyoen; tel: 3350 0151; www.env.go.jp/garden/shinjukugyoen; Tue–Sun 9am–4.30pm, last entry 4pm; charge). The lovely 60ha (150-acre) grounds, once part of the estate of the *daimyo* (feudal lord) Naito during the Edo period, only opened to the public in 1949. The park is divided into three sections: a northern section containing a garden in the formal French manner; a landscaped English garden at the centre; and a traditional Japanese garden, with winding paths, arched bridges, stone lanterns and artificial hills, in the southern section. Look out for the Taiwan-kaku Pavilion, a Chinese-style gazebo built to commemorate the wedding of the emperor Hirohito in 1927. The park's old botanical greenhouse, containing some splendid subtropical plants, is being rebuilt and should open again in 2011.

Hanazono-jinja
Retrace your steps to Isetan, walk along its eastern flank down Meiji-dori until you reach the wide boulevard called Yasukuni-dori. Cross it and turn left. Immediately on your right you will see the narrow entrance to the shrine **Hanazono-jinja** ⓭, an oasis of calm at the edge of one of Tokyo's raunchiest entertainment and red-light areas. The shrine dates back to the 6th century, but the current concrete-and-granite structure is more recent. One of the ubiquitous Inari fox shrines (Inari being a major fox deity and also messenger to Ebisu, the god of business and commerce), Hanazono is popular with local

Shinjuku Garden
This park is worth visiting in any season, but it's particularly beautiful in April, when acres of cherry-blossom trees are in full bloom, or in late October, when the autumn leaves are the attraction. Displays of chrysanthemums, the imperial flowers, are held during the first two weeks of November.

shopkeepers, who come here to pray for success in business. The vermillion-and-gold interior of the main hall is impressive. Stone lamps and spotlights come on at night, creating an enchanting atmosphere. A **flea market** is held in the grounds every Sunday.

Golden Gai

Shinjuku has a relationship with alcohol not unlike like that of Venice with water: it's built on it. Right next door to the shrine, forming a warren of narrow alleys with a grid of tiny two-storey bars, is **Golden Gai** ⓮ (www.golden gai.net), an endearing, retro crevice of Tokyo saved, for the time being, from the clutches of the speculator. Each of the some 200 bars in this area has a different clientele and most have a cover charge, to dissuade non-regulars, of anything from ¥1,000 to ¥4,000. One that is affordable is **Albatross G**, see ⑤; it's in the middle of the fifth alley from the southern end of Golden Gai.

Kabukicho

An attractive pedestrian pathway skirts the western side of Golden Gai to emerge just a few steps to the right of Kuyakusho-dori in the heart of **Kabukicho** ⓯. Tame-looking by day, the Kabukicho undergoes a transformation at twilight, when seedy hostess bars, strip joints, porno flea-pits, peep-shows and brothels (innocuously named 'Soap-lands') spark into neon-lit action. The area's linchpin, the **Koma Theatre** (Koma Gekijo) and neighbouring Toho Kaikan Building, closed in 2008 for major redevelopment, signalling a possible change of direction for the entertainment area. But for now you can still enjoy the lively atmosphere before heading back a few blocks south across Yasakuni-dori to Shinjuku Station.

Origin of Kabukicho
Kabukicho is so called because, after World War II, it was proposed that the destroyed Kabuki-za theatre be rebuilt here. In the end a new Kabuki-za resurfaced in Ginza, while this raunchy area of Shinjuku kept the classier-sounding name.

Left: Kabukicho hostess bars.

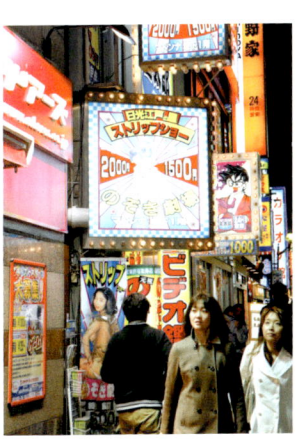

Food and Drink

④ TSUNAHACHI
3-31-8 Shinjuku, Shinjuku-ku; tel: 3352 1012; www.tunahachi.co.jp; daily 11am–10pm; ¥¥¥; station: Shinjuku
Hearty tempura (deep-fried battered seafood and vegetables) in large portions in an atmospheric wooden building. Good value and busy.

⑤ ALBATROSS G
2F 5th Ave, 1-1 Kabukicho, Shinjuku-ku; tel: 3202 3699; www.alba-s.com; Mon–Sat 8pm–5am; ¥¥; station: Shinjuku-Sanchome
There's only a ¥300 cover charge at this welcoming Golden Gai bar that's the sister operation of a slightly larger Albatross in Shomben Yokocho.

SHINJUKU NATIONAL GARDEN

YANAKA & UENO

On this walk through part of Tokyo's Shitamachi, or 'low city', Yanaka's atmospheric cemetery and Ameyoko's old black-market alleys sandwich the rich cultural attractions of Ueno Park, including the Tokyo National Museum.

DISTANCE 7.25km (4½ miles)
TIME A full day
START Nippori Station
END Ueno Station
POINTS TO NOTE
Ueno Park's museums could easily swallow up a day, so if you want to cover the rest of the walk, plan accordingly. Avoid doing this walk on Monday if you want to visit the museums, as this is when most of them are closed.

One of the few Tokyo districts to have come relatively unscathed through both the Great Kanto Earthquake of 1923 and the fire bombings of 1945, Yanaka has somehow also managed to avoid merciless redevelopment in the late 20th and early 21st centuries. This charmingly old-fashioned quarter, north of the Imperial Palace, dates from the Tokugawa Shogunate's decision to fortify the city's periphery with temples that would double as fortresses in the event of invasion.

Ueno Hill, where the giant temple Kan'ei-ji once stood, is now home to Ueno Park and several museums, including the outstanding Tokyo National Museum. The construction of a major railway terminus here in 1883 led to the arrival of millions of migrants from Japan's northeastern provinces in the post-war decades, resulting in a lively multicultural quarter.

Famous Graves

Among the some 7,000 graves at Yanaka Cemetery are those of several distinguished figures. At the graveyard offices (daily 8.30am–5.15pm) attendants will provide a map (in Japanese) and direct you to the last resting places of the composer and blind *koto*-player Miyagi Michio (1894–1956), the botanist Dr Makino Tomitaro (1862–1957), the well-known artist Yokoyama Taikan (1868–1958) and the female mass-murderer Takahashi Oden (1848–79). Japan's last shogun, Tokugawa Yoshinobu (1837–1913), is buried here too, alongside the ignominious and destitute whose unclaimed bodies were once requisitioned by Tokyo University as teaching aids for their medical faculty.

YANAKA CEMETERY AND ENVIRONS

Take the western exit from Nippori Station and follow the steps immediately on the left up to **Yanaka Cemetery ❶** (Yanaka Reien), one of the city's oldest graveyards, with mossy tombstones, leafy walks, wrought-iron gates and worn stone lanterns *(see feature, left)*.

Follow the stone path ahead until you reach the twin ancient wood and modern cement-and-steel gates to **Tenno-ji** ❷, a temple dating from the late 14th century. In its grounds you will find a serene-looking copper statue of Buddha crafted in 1690.

Asakura Choso Museum

Follow the main road south through the cemetery, turning right at the first crossroads to exit the grounds. At the T-junction beside the temple Choanji, turn right and follow the road until you reach, on the right, the **Asakura Choso Museum** ❸ (Asakura Chosokan; 7-18-10 Yanaka, Taito-ku; tel: 3821 4549; Tue–Thur, Sat–Sun 9.30am–4.30pm; charge), an excellent gallery dedicated to the artist Asakura Fumio (1883–1964), often described as the father of modern Japanese sculpture. The museum is based in Asakura's lovely studio-house, dating from 1935. The traditional garden to the rear of the house is of special interest, as stones around the pond have been arranged to reflect the Five Confucian Virtues, while the roof-garden provides panoramic views of the surrounding area.

Yanaka Ginza

Turn right out of the museum, then turn left at the junction with the road that runs back towards Nippori Station. Ahead, to the right of a fork in the road where there is a poodle parlour, a flight of steps leads down to the **Yanaka Ginza** ❹, a narrow shopping street with a retro atmosphere, full of small shops, cafés and traditional crafts stores.

Above from far left: traditional garden at the Asakura Choso Museum; sake barrels in Yanaka Ginza; gravestone, Yanaka Cemetery.

Above from left: *chiyogami* designs at Isetatsu; Tokyo National Museum; camellia *(tsubaki)* in Ueno Park.

ALONG SANSAKIZAKA

At the end of Yanaka Ginza turn left and continue ahead until the next major junction with Sansakizaka. Turn left here and head uphill to find, on the right, one of Tokyo's oldest and most exquisite paper-art shops, **Isetatsu** ❺ (2-18-9 Yanaka, Taito-ku; tel: 3823 1453; daily 10am–6pm), specialising in *chiyogami* – printed designs reproduced from original samurai textiles. Here you will find well-crafted fans, combs, dolls and colourful chests of drawers, all handmade from Japanese *washi* paper. Next door is the cosy **Yanaka Café**, see ⓘ①.

Daien-ji

Opposite Isetatsu and set back from the street is **Daien-ji** ❻, a temple that contains a monument to the charms of Osen, a teashop girl used by the artist Harunobu as a model for several of his woodblock prints. A statue of Kannon, the goddess of mercy, stands next to Osen's monument, and many Tokyoites, especially the elderly, make pilgrimages here to rub a spot on the statue that corresponds to the part of their body where they are suffering an ache or pain in the hope of a cure. If the more worn patches on this statue are anything to go by, stomach ailments and headaches are the most common complaints among Tokyo's senior citizens.

SCAI The Bathhouse

Continue up Sansakizaka until you reach Yanaka Cemetery again. Turn right and follow the road downhill to **SCAI The Bathhouse** ❼ (tel: 3821 1144; www.scaithebathhouse.com; Tue–Sat noon–7pm; free) on the right. The current building, dating from 1951, has been a contemporary-art gallery since 1993; for some 200 years before that, it was where the locals came to scrub and soak.

Yoshidaya Sake-ten

At the end of the road on the left is another evocative remnant of Tokyo's past, the **Yoshidaya Sake-ten** ❽ (tel: 3823 4408; Tue–Sun 9.30am–4.30pm; free). This merchant's shop, made from wood and dating from 1910, has been preserved as a museum just like it was in its heyday, with nostalgic posters, giant glass flasks and wooden barrels.

Right: paper-art shop, Isetatsu.

Turn right here and continue towards Nezu Station, about a five-minute walk down Kototoi-dori. Just on the left before reaching the station, take the side road to reach the entrance to the historic restaurant **Hantei**, see ①②.

JOMYO-IN

Backtrack from Hantei up Kototoi-dori until you eventually reach the temple **Jomyo-in** ❾ on the left; you will be greeted by a 20,000-strong army of tiny Jizo figures. A minor incarnation of the Buddha, Jizo is revered in Japan as a deity – the god of health and healing as well as protector of children. He is recognisable all over the country by his red-and-white bib and, in the case of the Jomyo-in, sponge gourds held in the left hand. Jizo statues are continually donated to the temple in the hope that one day they will reach their target of 84,000.

UENO PARK

Tokyo National Museum

A short walk along the road almost opposite the Jomyo-in carries you to the northwestern perimeter of **Ueno Park** (Ueno-koen). Here, the star attraction is the **Tokyo National Museum** ❿ (Tokyo Kokuritsu Hakubutsukan; tel: 3822 1111; www.tnm.go.jp; Tue–Sun 9.30am–5pm, Apr–Dec Fri until 8pm, Apr–Sept Sat–Sun until 6pm; charge), containing the most extensive collection of Japanese art in the world. The museum consists of four main galleries housed within buildings of various styles, including classic Japanese, ferro-concrete and European Beaux Arts. The central building, called the **Honkan**, contains the main permanent collection, a fine display of paintings, ceramics, lacquerware, calligraphy and textiles. Look out for *Pine Grove by the Seashore*, a six-panel gold-leaf screen from the 16th-century Muromachi period, and the consummate brush painting *Pine Trees* by the 16th-century artist Hasegawa Tohaku.

Leave time to explore the west gallery, the **Heisei-kan**, where there are archaeological relics such as funerary *haniwa* statues and, from the Jomon period, bug-eyed clay figures called *dogu*; and also the **Horyu-ji Homotsu-kan**, a newer hall containing priceless treasures from the Horyu-ji, a temple in Nara.

Park Walking Tours
Free 90-minute walking tours of Ueno Park are conducted in English by volunteers on Wed, Fri and Sun at 10.30am and 1.30pm. They depart from in front of the tourist information booth next to the National Museum of Western Art on the eastern side of the park.

Food and Drink

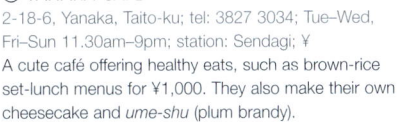

① YANAKA CAFÉ
2-18-6, Yanaka, Taito-ku; tel: 3827 3034; Tue–Wed, Fri–Sun 11.30am–9pm; station: Sendagi; ¥
A cute café offering healthy eats, such as brown-rice set-lunch menus for ¥1,000. They also make their own cheesecake and *ume-shu* (plum brandy).

② HANTEI
2-12-15 Nezu, Bunkyo-ku; tel: 3828 1440; Tue–Sat noon–2.30pm and 5–10pm, Sun until 9.30pm; station: Nezu; ¥¥¥
Kushiage (deep-fried skewers of fish, meat and vegetables) are served in a charming wooden building, constructed around a stone storehouse and located in one of Tokyo's best-preserved historic areas.

Blossom Viewing

Thousands of cherry trees make Ueno Park one of the most congested spots in the city during the spring cherry-blossom viewing season known as *hanami*.

Two Art Museums

A short stroll south across the park takes you to the **Tokyo Metropolitan Art Museum** ⓫ (Tokyo-to Bijutsukan; tel: 3823 6921; www.tobikan.jp; daily 9am–5pm; charge), where more than 2,600 works of mostly contemporary art are displayed in a light and spacious, partially underground, red-brick building. It is the work of architect Kunio Maekawa, who also designed the **Tokyo Metropolitan Festival Hall** (Tokyo Bunka Kaikan), where music concerts are held, and part of the **National Museum of Western Art** ⓬ (Kokuritsu Seiyo Bijutsukan; tel: 3828 5131; www.nmwa.go.jp; Tue–Sun 9.30am–5pm, Fri until 8pm; charge); both are on the park's eastern side. The original part of the Museum of Western Art, completed in 1959, is the work of Le Corbusier and its collection includes works by Renoir, Degas, Tintoretto and Rubens, as well as Miró, Picasso and Jackson Pollock. The courtyard has 57 Rodin sculptures.

Tosho-gu

Just past the Tokyo Metropolitan Art Museum is **Ueno Zoo** (Ueno Dobutsuen; tel: 3828 5171; www.tokyo-zoo.net; Tue–Sun 9.30am–5pm; charge), Japan's oldest zoo. South past the entrance is a stone *torii* leading to **Tosho-gu** ⓭, a shrine completed in 1651 and dedicated to the first shogun, Tokugawa Ieyasu. The approach to the shrine is lined with 200 stone lanterns, while fences on either side of the 'Chinese Gate' have superb carvings of fish, shells, birds and animals attributed to Hidari Jingoro, a brilliant Edo-period sculptor. According to legend, two realistic golden dragons which are carved onto the gate would slip off each night to drink from the waters of the nearby Shinobazu Pond.

Saigo Takamori Statue

Follow the paths under the trees past the wooden pillars of the **Kiyomizu Kannon-do**, a temple housing the Thousand-Armed Kannon, and stop for a moment to admire the large bronze statue of **Saigo Takamori** ⓮ on your left. Saigo (1827–73), one of the key architects of the Meiji Restoration, led an unsuccessful rebellion against its new leaders. He eventually committed ritual suicide. The statue

Right: Benten-do.

shows him dressed in a kimono walking his dog. Slightly northeast of the statue is the restaurant **Ito Ito**, see 🍴③.

Shinobazu Pond and Benten-do
Take the steps behind Kiyomizu Kannon-do leading down to **Shinobazu Pond** ⓯ (Shinobazu-no-ike). Once an inlet of Tokyo Bay, the pond is now split into three freshwater sections. The first, carpeted with lotus plants and reeds, is a sanctuary for many species of bird and fowl, including black cormorants, egrets, grebes and pintail ducks. The second part of the pond abuts Ueno Zoo, and the third is a small boating lake. A short causeway leads to **Benten-do** ⓰, an octagonal-roofed temple located on a small island. An eight-armed statue of Benzaiten, goddess of the arts, is enshrined here in the main hall.

Shitamachi Museum
Facing the southeastern corner of the pond is the interesting **Shitamachi Museum** ⓱ (Shitamachi Fuzoku Shiryokan; tel: 3823 7451; Tue–Sun 9.30am–4.30pm; charge). Extremely well designed, the museum evokes the huddled world of the common people who lived in the central areas of the city. Exhibits include utensils, tools, toys and furniture. There are also video presentations and photo exhibits, reconstructions of a merchant's house and narrow one-storey homes called *nagaya*. Near the museum you will find the venerable grilled-eel restaurant **Izuei**, see 🍴④.

AMEYA YOKOCHO

When you leave the museum, walk across Chuo-dori to the area slightly south of Ueno Station to find the entrance to the effervescent shopping street and market area called **Ameya Yokocho** ⓲. The name comes from the *ame*, meaning 'sweets', and *yokocho*, the word for 'alley', and it was a black-market zone for many years after World War II. Here, under the railway tracks, among the cheap clothes, fried-noodle vendors and dried-fish stalls, where young men hack blocks of ice and bellow the latest prices for strips of black seaweed, kelp and octopus, the working-class spirit of Shitamachi lives on.

Above from far left: Shinobazu Pond; lanterns strung among the trees.

Below: seaweed for sale at Ameya Yokocho market.

Food and Drink

③ ITO ITO
Bamboo Garden, 1-52 Ueno-koen, Taito-ku; tel: 5807 2244; Mon–Sat 11am–11.30pm, Sun 11am–11pm; station: Ueno; ¥¥

On the middle floor of the Bamboo Garden dining complex, where you will also find Korean and Chinese restaurants, Ito Ito serves a broad range of Japanese favourites, including *soba* noodles, *donburi* rice bowls and *sashimi* platters.

④ IZUEI
2-12-22 Ueno, Taito-ku; tel: 3831 0954; daily 11am–10pm; station: Ueno; ¥¥¥

Overlooking Shinobazu Pond, Izuei has been serving succulent *unagi* (grilled-eel) dishes for over 250 years. Sit at a table on the ground floor or on *tatami* mats on the upper levels.

IKEBUKURO & MEJIRODAI

Amble from the tranquil campus of a leafy Ivy League-style university to a classic Japanese garden, via the buzzing commercial heart of Ikebukuro and a cemetery that's the resting place of some of Japan's best-known literary figures.

DISTANCE 8km (5 miles)
TIME A leisurely day
START Ikebukuro Station
END Edogawabashi Station
POINTS TO NOTE
Do this walk at the weekend and you will be able to see kimono-dressed wedding parties enjoying the gardens at Chinzan-so.

The northwestern suburb of Ikebukuro, meaning 'pond hollow', started out as a marshy wetland of little consequence. The opening of a railway station here in 1903 and, later, the area's first department stores turned the district into a major transport and commercial hub. Today, Ikebukuro is the second-busiest commuter station in Japan after Shinjuku *(see p.50)*. The area around the station, dominated by big retail, is unexceptional compared to similar Tokyo mini-cities; instead, this walk takes you to off-the-beaten-path sights on Ikebukuro's periphery, then south towards a beautiful Japanese garden used as a backdrop for wedding photographs.

Station Shopping
Ikebukuro Station is dominated by the citadel-like flagship department stores of Seibu, which controls most of the eastern side of the station, and Tobu, whose domain lies to the west.

WEST IKEBUKURO

Exit on the west side of Ikebukuro Station – the Tobu side. Before escaping the department-store complex, head south to the attached Metropolitan Plaza building to find the **Japan Traditional Crafts Centre** ❶ (tel: 5954 6066; www.kougei.or.jp; daily 11am–7pm), with appealing handmade items from across the country, including ceramics, lacquerware and woodwork.

Two blocks west of Metropolitan Plaza is the **Tokyo Metropolitan Art Space** ❷ (Tokyo Geijutsu Gekijo; www.geigeki.jp; daily 9am–10pm), a concert, theatre and exhibition venue. Here a giant escalator carries visitors beneath a 28m (90ft) glass atrium up to a hallway with a colourful domed ceiling painted by Koji Kinutani.

Rikkyo University

Cross Gekijo-dori and carry on in a westerly direction through a warren of restaurants and bars, past a small park, until you come to the handsome red-brick gateway to **Rikkyo University** ❸, founded as St Paul's School in 1874 by an American missionary. Its ivy-covered buildings and white-clapboard New England-style faculty houses seem light years away from contemporary Ikebukuro. Stick your head into the main dining room, straight ahead from the entrance, to admire the vaulted wood-beam ceiling.

Jiyu Gakuen Myonichikan

Head back to Gekijo-dori, turn right and continue to the junction with the Ikebukuro Police Station. Cross the road and follow the side roads a few blocks south into a residential area to discover **Jiyu Gakuen Myonichikan** ❹ (tel: 3971 7535; www.jiyu.jp; Tue–Sun 10am–4.30pm; charge), the only Frank Lloyd Wright-designed building still standing in Tokyo. The Myonichikan (or 'House of Tomorrow') was originally home to the Jiyu Gakuen school. Appreciate the low-slung building's interior while sipping tea in its central hall. Weddings are often held here and at the chapel across the road at weekends.

Above from far left: commuters at Ikebukuro Station; prayer cards at Gokoku-ji; feline friend at Namco Namjatown theme park in Sunshine City; statues of monks at Gokoku-ji.

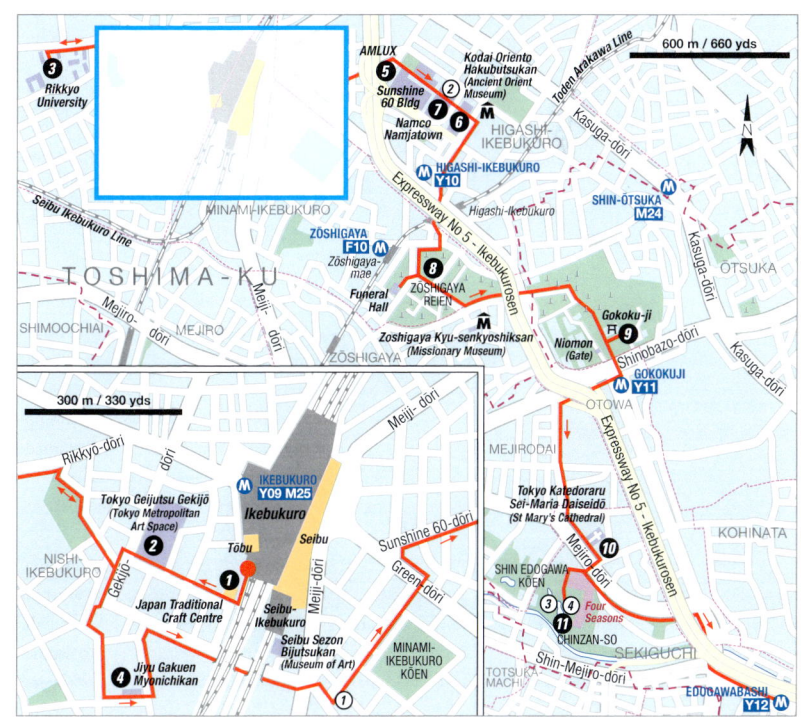

JIYU GAKUEN MYONICHIKAN **63**

EAST IKEBUKURO

Returning to the main road, turn right and head for the tunnel beneath the railway tracks, emerging on Meiji-dori. Cross over towards the Junku-do bookstore and walk one block behind it to find **Café Pause**, see ①.

From here head north to Green-dori, the main boulevard east from the station. Turn left, then right along the mainly pedestrian shopping street Sunshine 60-dori, past several cinemas and a branch of the handicrafts store Tokyu Hands. Just beyond the raised expressway is **AMLUX** ❺ (tel: 5391 5900; www.amlux.jp; Tue–Sun 11am–7pm; free), a high-tech Toyota showroom where you can play computer games featuring the company's racing cars.

Sunshine City

Opposite is the **Sunshine City** complex. Built in 1978, it includes a 60-floor tower, shopping malls, a hotel, theatre, planetarium, aquarium, kids' amusement park and viewing observatory, but looks dated in comparison with contemporary developments such as Tokyo Midtown and Roppongi Hills *(see p.37 and p.38)*. However, if you are interested in archaeology and ancient civilisations, visit the **Ancient Orient Museum** ❻ (Kodai Oriento Hakubutsukan; tel: 3989 3491; daily 10am–5pm; charge) on the seventh floor of Sunshine City's Bunka Kaikan section. Its collection of artefacts from the Indian Subcontinent and the Middle East includes objects excavated by Japanese teams before a dam was built on the Euphrates River.

If you have kids to entertain, or are looking for pop-cultural and culinary curiosities, while you are here stop at **Namco Namjatown** ❼ (tel: 5950 0765; www.namja.jp; daily 10am–10pm; charge), an inventively decorated indoor theme park notable for its **Ikebukuro Gyoza Stadium**, see ②, offering dumplings from chefs around Japan.

Food and Drink

① CAFÉ PAUSE
2-14-12 Minami-Ikebukuro, Toshima-ku; tel: 5950 6117; www.geocities.jp/cafe_pause_ikebukuro/; Mon–Sat noon–11pm, Sun noon–10pm; station: Ikebukuro; ¥
Contemporary pop culture infuses this laid-back café and gallery that hosts art exhibitions and events.

② IKEBUKURO GYOZA STADIUM
Namco Namjatown, 2F Sunshine City, 3-1 Higashi-Ikebukuro, Toshima-ku; tel: 5950 0765; www.namja.jp; daily 10am–10pm; station: Ikebukuro; ¥¥
After fried and boiled dumplings stuffed with prawns, beef, pork, and even kimchee (a Korean pickle) and cheese, go upstairs to Ice Cream City to taste an amazing range of flavours.

③ MUCHA-AN
Chinzan-so, 2-10-8 Sekiguchi, Bunkyo-ku; tel: 3943 1111; www.chinzanso.com; daily 11.30am–3.30pm and 5–9pm; station: Edogawabashi; ¥¥
Slurp hot or cold *soba* noodles – the duck *(kami)* soup ones are delicious – at this small restaurant tucked behind a bamboo grove in Chinzan-so.

④ KINSUI
Chinzan-so, 2-10-8 Sekiguchi, Bunkyo-ku; tel: 3943 1111; daily 2–6pm; station: Edogawabashi; ¥¥
Indulge in a traditional tea ceremony (¥1,500) in this lounge with a panoramic view across the gardens.

Zoshigaya Cemetry

Exit Sunshine City at its southeastern corner and continue south for about five minutes through the side streets towards the raised expressway and Higashi-Ikebukuro subway station, where you will also see the Toden Arakawa tram line. You can hop on the tram here for one stop to Zoshigaya or continue walking for another two minutes to reach **Zoshigaya Cemetery** ❽ (Zoshigaya Reien). This green and tranquil cemetery is the resting place of several well-known figures, including authors Natsume Soseki, Nagai Kafu and Lafcadio Hearn – pick up a map (in Japanese) from the Funeral Hall to locate their graves.

Gokoku-ji

Exit the cemetery at its eastern corner where you will again encounter the raised expressway. Go under, and on the other side you should find an open gate leading into another cemetery in the grounds of **Gokoku-ji** ❾ (tel: 3941 0764; www.gokokuji.or.jp). This well-preserved temple complex was established by the fifth shogun, Tokugawa Tsunayoshi, in 1681. The emperor Meiji (1852–1912) is buried here, as are several of his children. Exit the temple by its magnificent gate, Nio-mon, housing two fierce-looking statues placed at either side to ward off evil spirits. If you are tired, the entrance to Gokokuji subway station is also here.

MEJIRODAI

St Mary's Cathedral

Turn right from Gokoku-ji, head back under the expressway, take a left uphill and follow the backstreets south to Mejiro-dori, where you should take a left to arrive at **St Mary's Cathedral** ❿ (www.tokyo.catholic.jp; daily 9am–5pm) – its tall belltower should guide you. Designed by Kenzo Tange in 1964, the seat of Tokyo's Roman Catholic church, like the architect's Olympic stadium in Yoyogi *(see p.45)*, still appears strikingly modern. The interior is dominated by a gigantic pipe organ, the largest of its kind in Japan, on which concerts are occasionally given.

Chinzan-So

Opposite the cathedral, a wedding hall and the Four Seasons Hotel share the view across the lovely garden of **Chinzan-so** ⓫ (tel: 3943 1111; www.chinzanso.com; daily 9am–8pm; free). Meaning 'House of Camellia', the garden, designed in the late 19th century, includes a 1,000-year-old pagoda that originally hails from a temple in Hiroshima Prefecture, ancient stone lanterns and monuments, and several restaurants including **Mucha-an**, see ⑪③. There's also **Kinsui**, see ⑪④, where you can partake in a traditional tea ceremony. From Chinzan-so, it's around a 10-minute walk downhill back towards the raised expressway to find the entrance to Edogawabashi Station.

Above from far left: arcade racing at Namco Namjatown; St Mary's Cathedral.

Tokyo Tramway

Central Tokyo's sole remaining tramway is the Toden Arakawa line, running between Waseda and Minowa-bashi. Tickets cost ¥160 however far you travel on the line. The stretch between Higashi-Ikebukuro and Shin-Koshinzuka stations (the latter next to Nishi-Sugamo station on the Toei Mita line) will give you a good taste of what public transport in Tokyo used to be like.

ASAKUSA

Experience the lively atmosphere around one of Tokyo's most famous temples on this walk through Asakusa, followed by a short cruise down the Sumida River to a beautiful bayside garden.

DISTANCE 4km (2½ miles)
TIME 6 hours
START/END Asakusa Station
POINTS TO NOTE
If you take the river cruise at the end of this walk to Hama Rikyu Teien, then the closest subway station is Tsukiji-Shijo, from where you can follow the itinerary through Tsukiji Fish Market and across to Tsukudajima (see p.76).

This traditional Tokyo district, northeast of the Imperial Palace and centred around the major Buddhist temple Senso-ji, has retained the bustling commerce and ribald good humour that made it the heart of the Edo-era Shitamachi ('low city'). Festivals are constantly celebrated here *(see feature, p.69)*, and it's a great area for traditional craft and souvenir stores. To the west you can shop for kitchenware in Kappabashi, while to the east is the Sumida River, ideal for a cruise to finish off.

Visitor Information

The Asakusa Tourist Information Centre (tel: 3842 5566; daily 9.30am–8pm) is opposite the Kaminarimon. Drop by to find out what's going on in the area and to join a one-hour guided walking tour of Senso-ji and the surrounding area (Sun 11am and 2pm; free).

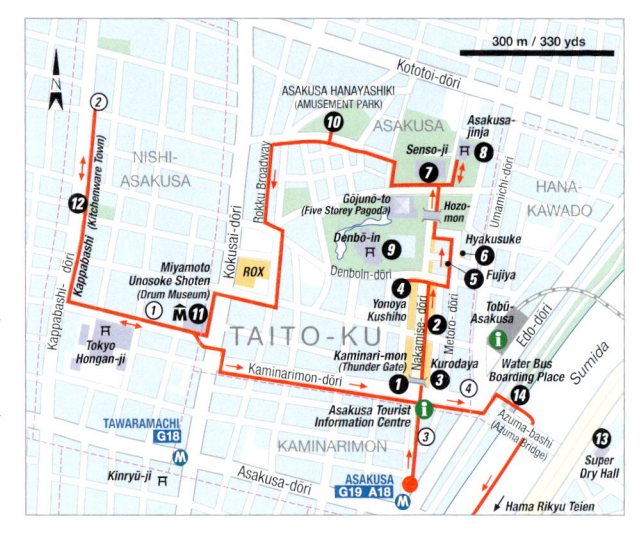

SENSO-JI

Enshrining a golden statue of Kannon, goddess of mercy – said to have been fished out of the nearby river in 628AD – Senso-ji is Asakusa's spiritual centre. The temple's central compound is best approached after passing under the **Kaminari-mon** ❶ (Thunder Gate), an impressive wooden entrance flanked by leering twin meteorological deities (Fujin, god of wind, on the right, and Raijin, god of thunder, on the left) and a magnificent giant red paper lantern with the character for 'thunder' emblazoned across it.

Nakamise-dori

Stretching for about 400m/yds from Kaminari-mon to Senso-ji's main hall of worship is **Nakamise-dori** ❷, a perpetually thronged avenue of colourful stalls selling an amazing variety of products, from the traditional (rice crackers and paper fans) to the bizarre (clothes for dogs).

Either side of Nakamise-dori you will find more of the traditional craft shops that make browsing around Asakusa such a pleasure. Beside Kaminari-mon to the right is **Kurodaya** ❸ (tel: 3844 7511; Tue–Sun 11am–7pm); in business since 1856, the shop sells traditional woodblock prints and *washi* paper products.

Where Nakamise-dori crosses Denboin-dori, turn left to find **Yonoya Kushiho** ❹ (tel: 3844 1755; Thur–Tue 10.30am–6pm) on the left. The shop is much sought out for its traditional hairpieces, ornaments and exquisite boxwood combs.

Now head right from Nakamise-dori along Denboin-dori and turn left up Metoro-dori to arrive at **Fujiya** ❺ (tel: 3841 2283; Thur–Tue 10am–6pm), specialising in *tenugui* (hand-printed towels with original designs). A little further up, to the right, **Hyakusuke** ❻ (tel: 3841 7058; Wed–Mon 11am–5pm) is another esoteric shopping experience, having supplied local geisha and *kabuki* actors with cosmetics for more than 100 years. Among its refined goods is a skin cream made from the powdered droppings of the Japanese nightingale.

The Central Compound

At the head of Nakamise-dori, a second gate, the imposing doublestoreyed **Hozo-mon**, disgorges visitors into the wide open grounds that surround the **Senso-ji** ❼ (www.senso-ji.jp). Acrid clouds of incense waft from a large bronze burner that stands here. Visitors immerse themselves and their clothing in this 'breath of the gods' before mounting the broad stoneflagged steps that lead to the temple's main Kannondo hall.

Behind Kannondo, the **Asakusajinja** ❽ is dedicated to the fishermen brothers who found the Kannon statue back in the 7th century and their lord Haji-no-Nakatomo, who built the

Above: Kaminarimon or Thunder Gate.

Below: details from the Senso-ji compound.

Above from left: Nakamise-dori; Azuma Bridge and the Super Dry Hall topped by La Flamme d'Or.

original hall to enshrine it in 645. Sadly, this remarkable golden image has remained hidden away in the inner recesses of Senso-ji ever since.

The western half of the Senso-ji compound houses **Gojuno-to**, an impressive 1973 reconstruction of a five-storey pagoda first built at the temple in 942. Its towering vermilion outline stands beside the **Denbo-in** ❾, the residence of Senso-ji's head priest. The building itself is closed to the public, but check to see whether access is permitted to the garden, with its classic view of the pagoda reflected in a pond, at the small booth just left of the pagoda.

ASAKUSA HANAYASHIKI

West of Senso-ji lies Asakusa's raunchy entertainment district. Adult cinemas, strip clubs, old-fashioned public baths and street barkers are some of the features here. Another local institution is the rickety amusement park **Asakusa Hanayashiki** ❿ (tel: 3842 8780; daily 10am–6pm; charge). Dating from 1872, most of the rides and game machines here seem to have a certain vintage quality about them. The park claims to have hosted Japan's first rollercoaster in 1953, and there's also an eerie *obakiyashiki* (ghost house).

DRUM MUSEUM

Just west of the amusement park, turn left and follow Rokku Broadway, a shopping street that runs parallel to the main Kokusai-dori. After you pass the department store ROX, turn right to the main road. Cross over and turn left to reach **Miyamoto Unosuke Shoten** ⓫ (tel: 3874 4131; www.miyamoto-unosuke.co.jp; Wed–Mon 9am–6pm), a shop with a huge collection of tradi-

---

Food and Drink

① SOMETARO
2-2-2 Nishi-Asakusa, Taito-ku; tel: 3844 9502; daily noon–10.30pm; station: Tawaramachi; ¥¥
There are often lines of people waiting outside this rustic eatery, where the speciality is *okonomiyaki*, batter pancakes stuffed with vegetables, shrimp, etc, and covered with lashings of soy sauce and mayonnaise.

② KAPPABASHI COFFEE
3-25-11 Nishi-Asakusa, Taito-ku; tel: 3843 9555; daily 10am–7pm; station: Tawaramachi; ¥
A sophisticated café at the northern end of Kappabashi-dori, serving good coffee, tea and other drinks, as well as cakes and light meals.

③ GALLERY ÉF
2-19-18 Kaminari-mon, Taito-ku; tel: 3841 0442; www.gallery-ef.com; Wed–Mon café and gallery 11am–7pm, bar 6pm–midnight; station: Asakusa; ¥¥
A trendy café-bar based around a stone-walled *kura* (traditional storehouse), dating from 1868, which is used for art exhibitions. A coffee and cake set menu is ¥750.

④ KAMIYA
1-1-1 Asakusa, Taito-ku; tel: 3841 5400; www.kamiya-bar.com; Wed–Mon 11.30am–10pm; station: Asakusa; ¥¥
In business since 1880, Tokyo's first Western-style bar is famous for its Denkibran ('Electric Brandy') – a stimulating concoction of gin, wine, curaçao and brandy. On the informal ground floor you pay for your food and drinks at the cash desk as you enter, while upstairs it's table service.

tional Japanese festival wear and musical instruments. On the store's fourth floor an impressive display of percussion instruments constitutes the **Drum Museum** (tel: 3842 5622; Wed–Sun 10am–5pm; charge); you can try many of the drums out yourself. Around the corner, to the right, is the popular *okonomiyaki* restaurant **Sometaro**, see ⃝①.

KAPPABASHI

From Sometaro, keep walking a few blocks west past the rear of the temple Tokyo Hongan-ji to reach Kappabashi-dori, the heart of **Kappabashi** ⓬ or Kitchenware Town, a wholesale restaurant equipment area. If you have ever wondered where those life-like plastic food displays in restaurant windows come from, here is your answer. A great café to relax in is **Kappabashi Coffee**, see ⃝②, a few blocks north along Kappabashi-dori.

SUPER DRY HALL

Return to Kaminarimon-dori and continue to the Sumida River; you can grab a drink nearby at either **Gallery éf**, see ⃝③, or the venerable bar **Kamiya**, see ⃝④. On the other side of the Azuma Bridge (Azuma-bashi) stands one of Tokyo's wackiest pieces of architecture – **Super Dry Hall** ⓭ (tel: 5608 5381; daily 11.30am–10pm), a beer hall designed by Philippe Starck for the Asahi Beer Company. More a sculpture than a building, it has a massive black base polished like a tombstone and is topped with a giant golden structure called La Flamme d'Or.

SUMIDA RIVER CRUISE

Beside Azuma-bashi you can board one of the **Sumida River double-decker river buses** ⓮ (tel: 0120-977 311; www.suijobus.co.jp; daily 9.45am–6.30pm; charge), known as *suijyo basu*, which depart roughly every 30 minutes. It's a 35-minute journey south along the river to the beautifully laid-out **Hama Rikyu Garden** (Hama Rikyu Teien; Tue–Sun 9am–4.30pm; charge), a former imperial duck shoot that sports a lovely traditional teahouse and wisteria trellises that look magnificent in spring. From the garden, it's a short walk to either Ginza *(see p.35)* or Tsukiji Fish Market *(see p.74)*.

Below: Kappabashi kitchenware.

> ## Asakusa's Festivals
>
> One of Tokyo's top festivals, the three-day Sanja Matsuri, held on the third weekend in May, sees Asakusa's streets jam-packed as over 100 ornate *mikoshi* (portable shrines) are danced around. It's equally busy in late July when all of Tokyo, dressed in summer *yukata* (cloth robes), descend to watch the spectacular *hanabi* (fireworks) contests held along the Sumida River. As the summer heat reaches its peak at the end of August, Asakusa comes over all Brazilian with a samba carnival (www.asakusa-samba.jp) parading through the streets.

FUKAGAWA & RYOGOKU

On the eastern side of the Sumida River is little-visited Fukagawa, where you will find a traditional garden, contemporary art galleries and lively temples and shrines, as well as Ryogoku, home to the national sport of sumo wrestling.

DISTANCE 5km (3 miles)
TIME A leisurely day
START Kiyosumi-Shirakawa Station
END Ryogoku Station
POINTS TO NOTE
The above distance doesn't include the subway ride from Monzen-Nakacho and Ryogoku, which is about 3km (2 miles). Avoid doing this walk in Monday if you want to visit the art galleries and museums.

Relatively few visitors to Tokyo make it east across the Sumida River, even though the area is steeped in history and has a relaxed old Edo atmosphere and some notable sights. Not only does the district of Fukagawa have interesting temples, shrines and a traditional garden, but it is also making waves on the contemporary art scene as new galleries open up in empty riverside warehouses. North of Fukagawa is Ryogoku, a district primarily associated with sumo wrestling thanks to its being the location of the National Sumo Stadium. It's also where you can find a wonderful museum devoted to the city's history.

Fukagawa History

The area gets its name from the late 16th-century local leader Fukagawa Hachiroemon, who was granted the land by Tokugawa Ieyasu and charged with draining and filling in the swamp that once existed here. In the late 17th century, following one of Tokyo's perennial fires, the area began to boom, as lumber yards were relocated here and new bridges over the Sumida River facilitated commerce between the two sides of the city. At the same time, the area also became one of the city's 'unlicensed' quarters where brothels, masquerading as teahouses, plied their business – a trade that continued right up to and a few years beyond World War II.

FUKAGAWA

Fukagawa Edo Museum
Start at the **Fukagawa Edo Museum** ❶ (Fukagawa Edo Shiryokan; 1-3-28 Shirakawa, Koto-ku; tel: 3630 8625; daily 9.30am–5pm; charge), a block directly south of Kiyosumi-Shirakawa Station (take exit A3), where you can experience Fukagawa *circa* 1842, with evocative displays of homes, shops, a theatre, a boathouse tavern and even a 10m (33ft) fire tower.

Reigan-ji

The shopping street leading to the museum is charming. It features **Reigan-ji** ❷, a temple dating from 1624, which is best known for its early 18th-century bronze statue of a Jizo figure, seated on a lotus pedestal, and an award-winning public toilet with an Edo-era façade.

Kiyosumi Garden

Return to the crossroads, where Kiyosumi-dori and Kiyosubashi-dori intersect. Cross the road and follow Kiyosubashi-dori to the entrance to the beautiful **Kiyosumi Garden** ❸ (Kiyosumi Teien; tel: 3641 5892; daily 9am–5pm; charge). This spacious classic *sukiya*-style garden, dating back to the Edo period and designed around a central pond, features an exquisite teahouse that appears to float majestically above the water. Look out for the 55 rare stones gathered from all over Japan by Iwasaki Yataro, the founder of Mitsubishi, who acquired the gardens in the 19th century.

Zenshi Galleries

Exit the gardens and cross the adjacent public park heading towards the road beside the 24-hour Times parking lot. About 100m/yds down towards the river, an unlikely-looking warehouse is the location of **Zenshi** ❹ (Tue–Sat noon–7pm; free), which is a collection of six contemporary art galleries spread across three floors. Here you will find **Tomio Koyama Gallery** (tel: 3642 4090; www.tomiokoyamagallery.com) and **Shugo Arts** (tel: 5621 6434; www.shugoarts.com), both specialising in fine arts, and **Taka Ishii Gallery** (tel: 5646 6050; www.takaishiigallery.com), which displays photographs.

Three Bridges

From Zenshi you are steps away from the Sumida River, the setting for what is one of the most interesting concentrations of bridges in Japan. A strong nostalgia is attached to these spans, and Tokyoites continue to celebrate them in songs, watercolours, films and novels. First up is the blue-painted **Kiyosu-bashi** ❺, a handsome suspension bridge

Above from far left: Kiyosu-bashi; sumo wrestling motif by the Sumida River.

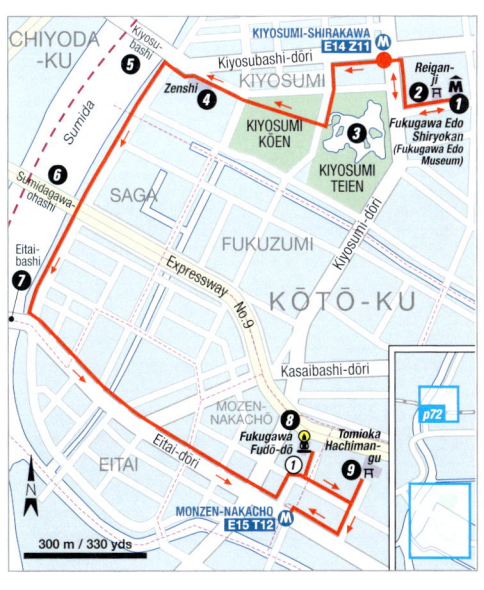

Waterbuses

The Tokyo Mizubi line (tel: 5608 8869; www.tokyo-park.or.jp) waterbuses, which travel along the Sumida River, out into Tokyo Bay and over to Odaiba *(see p.78)*, can be caught from opposite the National Sumo Stadium.

Fukagawa Market

A lively flea market, the Fukagawa *ennichi* is held three Sundays a month in the grounds of the shrine Tomioka Hachiman-gu.

---

built in 1928. From here, follow the riverside promenade south to **Sumida-gawa-ohashi** ❻; the bridge itself is unattractive due to the flyover above it, but there are great views up- and downstream. Continue for a few minutes until the more graceful blue girders of the 1926 **Eitai-bashi** ❼, one of the oldest bridges on the river, come into view.

Fukagawa Fudo-do

Staying on this side of the river, walk east along Eitai-dori for about 900m/yds until you reach the shopping parade around Monzen-Nakacho Station. Cross Kiyosumi-dori and turn left to find **Fukagawa Fudo-do** ❽, a busy temple of the Shingon sect of Buddhism. The original early 18th-century temple was destroyed in World War II; this one, dating from 1862, was transported here from Chiba Prefecture outside of Tokyo. The narrow shopping street leading to the temple from exit 1 of Monzen-Nakacho Station is lined with small restaurants and stalls selling *senbei* rice crackers. Try **Kintame**, see ⓘ①, opposite the temple.

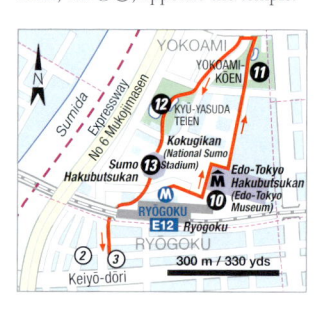

Tomioka Hachiman-gu

Just east of the temple is the **Tomioka Hachiman-gu** ❾, a shrine that is the focus of one of Tokyo's greatest festivals, the mid-August Fukagawa Matsuri. A 1968 reconstruction of the 17th-century original, the current shrine has impressive prayer and spirit halls and a towering green copper-tiled roof. It is dedicated to eight deities, including Benten, goddess of beauty and the arts.

The shrine is strongly associated with sumo wrestling and in the Edo era was the official venue for the sport. Walk to the back of the shrine and you will see the **Yokozuna Monument**, engraved with the names of long-departed sumo wrestlers who reached the rank of *ozeki*, the highest in the sumo world.

Exit through the shrine's main *torii* gate, and turn right to reach the subway at Monzen-Nakacho. Take the Oedo line three stops north to Ryogoku.

RYOGOKU

Edo-Tokyo Museum

Behind the station exit is the impressive **Edo-Tokyo Museum** ❿ (Edo-Tokyo Hakubutsukan; 1-4-1 Yokoami, Sumida-ku; tel: 3626 9974; www.edo-tokyo-museum.or.jp; Tue–Sun 9.30am–5.30pm, Sat until 7.30pm; charge), based in a wedge-shaped monolith balanced on four massive pillars. Highlights of the museum, which traces the history of the city from its founding through to the post-war reconstruction years, are replicas of the Nihonbashi, the wooden bridge which stood at the centre of Edo, the residence of a *daimyo* (feudal lord) and a *kabuki* stage.

Yokoami Park

One block north of the museum is small **Yokoami Park** ⓫ (Yokoami-koen), in which the austere temple-like complex of **Tokyo Ireido** is dedicated to the 100,000 victims of the Great Kanto Earthquake which struck just before noon on 1 September 1923 and destroyed over 70 percent of Tokyo. A small **museum** (tel: 3622 1208; Tue–Sun 9am–5pm; charge) displays remains from the fateful day.

Kyu-Yasuda Garden

Leave the park by the west gate behind Tokyo Ireido and cross diagonally to reach the small but distinguished **Kyu-Yasuda Garden** ⓬ (Kyu-Yasuda Teien; daily 9am–4.30pm; free). Preserving the spirit of an old Edo-period stroll garden, the grounds were acquired in the 1850s by wealthy industrialist and banker Yasuda Zenjiro, grandfather of the avant-garde artist and musician Yoko Ono.

National Sumo Stadium

Immediately south of the garden is the **National Sumo Stadium** ⓭ (Kokugikan; tel: 3622 1100). Two-week stints of this highly ritualised, visually pleasing sport are held here in January,

May and September. There is a small **Sumo Museum** (Sumo Hakubutsukan; Mon–Fri 10am–4.30pm; free) on the same premises.

One of the ways in which sumo wrestlers acquire such giant girths is by consuming bowls of a nutritious, but body-enriching, stew called *chanko-nabe*. If you would like to sample the dish yourself, several restaurants in the area specialise in it. One of the best is **Chanko Kawasaki**, see ②, housed in an atmospheric 1937 building; another is **Tomoegata**, see ③.

Above from far left: Edo-Tokyo Museum; packed-out National Sumo Stadium.

Food and Drink

① KINTAME

1-14-3 Tomioka, Koto-ku; tel: 3641 4561; www.kintame.co.jp; Tue–Sun 11am–5pm; station: Monzen-Nakacho; ¥¥
Opposite the Fukagawa Fudo-do temple, this appealing place serves tasty Kyoto-style fish marinated in sake lees (deposits produced during fermentation), and a variety of pickles.

② CHANKO KAWASAKI

2-13-1 Ryogoku, Sumida-ku; tel: 3631 2529; Mon–Sat 5–9pm; station: Ryogoku; ¥¥
Like many others in the area, this restaurant specialises in *chanko-nabe* stews, but it has the edge because of its location in a charming post-World War II wooden house and its friendly owners. A set meal starts at ¥3,050, and bookings are advised as it's pretty small.

③ TOMOEGATA

2-17-6 Ryogoku, Sumida-ku; tel: 3632 5600; www.tomoegata.com; daily 11.30am–2pm and 5–11pm; station: Ryogoku; ¥¥
Fluttering colourful banners mark the exterior of this restaurant, with branches either side of the road, where you can sample the sumo wrestlers' favourite stew, *chanko-nabe*. If you are not so hungry, then the ¥840 *sebisu-chanko* (only served for lunch Monday to Friday) will suffice.

TSUKIJI & TSUKUDAJIMA

Get up early to watch Tsukiji Fish Market in full flight and have a fantastically fresh sushi breakfast, then pay a visit to charming Tsukudajima, a tiny enclave that evokes the Tokyo of centuries ago.

DISTANCE 5km (3 miles)
TIME A half day
START Tsukiji-shijo Station
END Tsukishima or Toyosu stations
POINTS TO NOTE
Check Tsukiji's website first for the calendar of when it's open – there are often holidays in addition to the regular Sunday closing. Tsukiji has become so popular that rules for visitors have been introduced; indeed, at one point in 2008 tourists were banned from the tuna auctions for interfering with the work of legitimate buyers – if you do attend an auction, be aware that this is a place of business. For late risers, a visit to the market is still worth it, but note that the stalls start winding down at midday. Water-resistant, rubber-soled footwear is recommended, as the floors at Tsukiji are wet and slippery. Toyosu is also the terminus for the Yurikamome monorail through Odaiba *(see p.78)* should you wish to visit that area in the afternoon.

Below: produce at the Fish Market.

The earlier in the morning you can start the better for this walk, which kicks off at the Tokyo Metropolitan Central Wholesale Market, better known as the Tsukiji Fish Market. Selling a diverse range of fresh produce as well as fish, the market – the biggest of its kind in the world – is one of Tokyo's main tourist attractions and certainly worth seeing in action. There's plenty going on at the market and the surrounding area; if you head here later in the day, a leisurely stroll along the mouth of the Sumida River and over to the island of Tsukudajima is recommended.

TSUKIJI FISH MARKET

Six days a week, almost 3,000 tonnes of seafood from all around the world arrive at **Tokyo Metropolitan Central Wholesale Market** ❶ (Tokyo Chuo Oroshiurishijo or Tsukiji-shijo; www.tsukiji-market.or.jp; Mon–Sat 3am–noon, check website for occasional holidays) for sorting, auctioning and dispatching. Wholesalers start laying out their stalls and preparing for the 5.30am tuna auction in the dead of night. The best cuts of these rock-hard fish, lined up like frozen sputniks and marked in red paint with their country of origin and weight, sell wholesale for as much as ¥10,000 per kilo, several times the price of the most expensive prime beef. At 7am the fruit and vegetable auctions start, and Tsukiji keeps buzzing until noon as vendors hawk some 450 different types of fish.

Sushi Breakfast

With all this fresh seafood on tap, Tsukiji is an excellent place to indulge in a sushi breakfast: in the Outer Market (Jogai-shijo) you will find a cluster of stalls selling sushi and other dishes made with seafood. One of the best is **Sushi Bun**, see ①①, or you could try a seafood *donburi* (rice bowl) at **Kanno**, see ①②.

TSUKIJI HONGAN-JI

Leaving the market, follow Shin-Ohashi-dori across Harumi-dori to see the distinctive **Tsukiji Hongan-ji** ❷ (tel: 3541 1131; www.tsukiji hongwanji.jp), one of the most unusual temples in Tokyo. Dating from 1935, it was designed by Ito Chuta, who wished to stress the link between Japanese Buddhism and its Indian origins.

Take a peek into the interior, with its opulent gold altar and elaborately carved transoms, which can seat up to 1,000 people.

TSUKIJI JISAKU

Return to the crossing with Harumi-dori and walk southeast towards the river. Turn left at the road just before the Kachidoki Bridge (Kachidoki-bashi) and walk towards St Luke's Hospital. Just before reaching it you will see **Tsukiji Jisaku**, see ①③, an exclusive banqueting restaurant in the former home of Mitsubishi group founder Iwasaki Yataro. The lush entrance is a foretaste of the traditional gardens that several of the mansion's rooms overlook.

Above from far left: freshly caught octopus; tuna auction.

Food and Drink

① SUSHI BUN

5 Tsukiji, Chuo-ku; tel: 3541 3860; Mon–Sat 6am–2.30pm; closed during occasional market hols; station: Tsukiji-shijo; ¥¥¥

The original Sushi Bun opened over 150 years ago when the fish market was at Nihonbashi. The same family still run it in its present location within the market complex. There's an English menu, and set menus start from around ¥2,100.

② KANNO

4-9-5 Tsukiji, Chuo-ku; tel: 3541 9191; daily 5am–3.30pm; station: Tsukiji-shijo; ¥¥

Facing Shin-Ohashi-dori, this simple stall with roadside seating dishes up *donburi* (rice bowls) topped with creamy *uni* (sea urchin), *ikura* (salmon roe) and *maguro* (tuna) at bargain prices.

③ TSUKIJI JISAKU

14-19 Akashicho, Chuo-ku; tel: 3545 2182; www.jisaku. co.jp; Mon–Fri 5–10pm, Sat 11am–10pm, Sun 11am–6pm; station: Tsukiji; ¥¥¥¥

If you have guests to impress, come to this elegant, traditional mansion with manicured-garden views and waitresses in kimonos serving *kaiseki ryori* – Japanese haute cuisine.

TSUKUDAJIMA

A riverside walkway runs from beside St Luke's Hospital to the Tsukuda Bridge (Tsukuda-ohashi) across to the island of **Tsukudajima**. Meaning 'Island of Cultivated Rice Fields', the name is a reference to the rural outskirts of Osaka, from where its first settlers came in the 17th century to work as primarily as fishermen, supplying the shogun's kitchens with fish, but also as watchmen, keeping an eye on movements in Edo's bay.

By the early Meiji period, Tsukudajima had been combined with the reclaimed islands of Ishikawajima to the north and Tsukishima to the south in one contiguous landfill. Spared the great fires of Edo and the earthquake that struck Tokyo in 1923, the island's huddles of housing blocks, narrow alleyways full of potted plants and old-fashioned street-corner lift-pumps (some still in use) lend Tsukudajima its distinctive character. Many of the houses have traditionally crafted features, including black ceramic roofs, oxidised copper finials of an ancient green patina and well-seasoned wooden walls.

Food and Drink
④ RI JAN

1-6-7 Tsukuda, Chuo-ku; tel: 3531 6631; daily 11.30am–2.30pm and 5–9.30pm; station: Tsukukishima; ¥
Look for the ceramic pickling jars lined up outside this cosy Chinese restaurant beside the Tsukudako Bridge. They do a set lunch for ¥1,000.

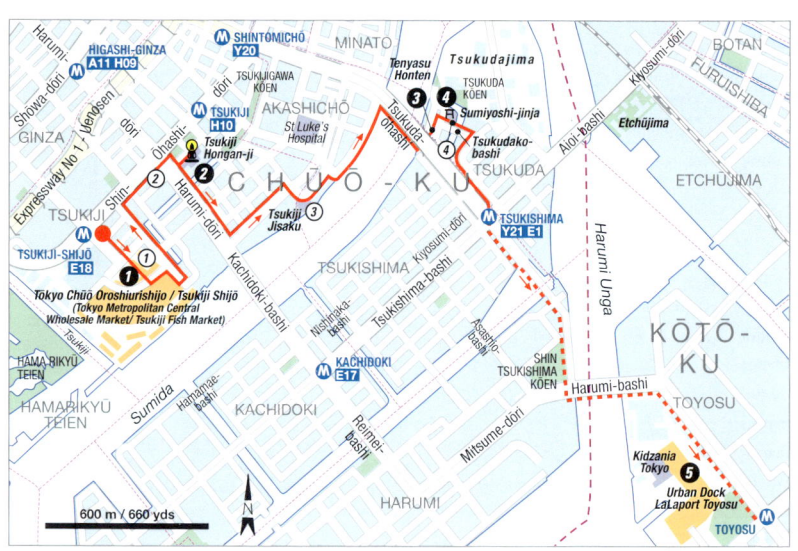

Above from far left: Tsukudako Bridge; high-rise Toyosu.

Tenyasu Honten

To see one such house, after crossing the bridge take the stairs down to the left to find **Tenyasu Honten** ❸ (tel: 3531 2351; daily 9am–6pm), a charming shop selling one of the island's best-known products – *tsukudani* (seaweed and fish preserve in a preparation of salt, soy sauce and sugar). A sampler box of six types of *tsukudani*, which tastes great with rice, costs ¥2,000.

Sumiyoshi-jinja

In days of old, visitors to the island brought offerings of *tsukudani* to the **Sumiyoshi-jinja** ❹, less than a minute's walk away to the right and then to the left. Vestiges of the shrine's role as a protector of sea travellers, fishermen and sailors can be seen in carvings on beams and transoms covering some of the small outer buildings. One particularly realistic relief on the roof of the well beside the shrine's *torii* shows fishermen in a skiff, with firewood burning in a metal basket as they cast their nets into the bay at night.

A few steps beyond the shrine, **Tsukudako Bridge** (Tsukudako-bashi) is an attractive bridge with a red handrail that spans a narrow tidal inlet where you can get a modest insight into the former life of this quarter. The fishermen's shacks and boathouses are less charmingly dilapidated than they were just a few years ago, and the number of their vessels is depleted. Nearby is the Chinese restaurant **Ri Jan**, see ❹.

URBAN DOCK LALAPORT TOYOSU

Turn right after the bridge and head southeast towards Tsukishima Station, where you can end this walk. Alternatively, take the subway one stop east to Toyosu (or walk there – it's about 1.5km/1 mile) to check out the future location of the Tokyo Metropolitan Central Wholesale Market and to cruise the 21st-century retail experience that is **Urban Dock LaLaport Toyosu** ❺ (http://toyosu.lalaport.jp; daily 10am–9pm). Alongside the shops, restaurants and multiplex cinema here, you will find **Ukiyo-e Tokyo** (Tue–Fri noon–7pm, Sat–Sun 11am–7pm; charge), a small exhibition of traditional woodblock prints, and **Kidzania Tokyo** (www.kidzania.jp; daily 10am–3pm, 4–10pm; charge), an interior theme park where children get to run a small fantasy town.

Tsukiji on the Move

The name Tsukiji means 'reclaimed land'. The shogun ordered a landfill to be made here in 1657 after that year's disastrous Furisode (Long Sleeves) Fire. During the early Meiji years some vaguely European-looking wooden houses were built at Tsukiji for the foreigners who worked in the newly opened legations, trading houses and missionary enterprises. The market moved from its former home in Nihonbashi to Tsukiji in 1935. Since the current cramped location has become outdated, the authorities plan for it to move again, most likely in 2012, to a new facility being built on a patch of reclaimed land in Toyosu, 1.5km (1 mile) across Tokyo Bay.

ODAIBA

Ride the monorail out into Tokyo Bay to explore this man-made island of futuristic buildings, interesting museums and quirky shopping malls. Finish with a bath at a hot-spring complex and a walk across the Rainbow Bridge.

Reclaimed City
Landfills in Tokyo Bay have been adding new dimensions to the city's compressed urban landscape for more than 400 years. The island of Odaiba, which started to be developed in earnest in the late 1980s, has become a laboratory for outsized architectural projects that require more space than central Tokyo is capable of providing.

DISTANCE 7.5km (4¾ miles)
TIME A half day
START Kokusai-Tenjijo-Seimon Station/Tokyo Big Sight
END Shibaura-Futo Station
POINTS TO NOTE
A ¥800 one-day ticket for the Yurikamome monorail (www.yurikamome.co.jp), connecting with Tokyo's subway at Shimbashi and Toyosu stations, lets you hop on and off at will. Odaiba is often deserted in the week, but usually busy at weekends.

TOKYO BIG SIGHT

Heading by monorail to the east of the island of Odaiba, you can't fail to miss the gravity-defying **Tokyo Big Sight** ❶ (www.bigsight.jp), a massive convention centre housing exhibition halls, meeting rooms, restaurants and cafés. It consists of four inverted pyramids standing on a deceptively small base and is best accessed from Kokusai-Tenjijo-Seimon monorail station, outside of which there's a puzzling sculpture depicting a huge upended saw.

Below: Odaiba's saw sculpture.

PALETTE TOWN

Follow the monorail tracks southwest in the direction of a highly visible Ferris wheel – the **Giant Sky Wheel** (charge); this looks best at night, when it glows in a rainbow of colours. The wheel is part of **Palette Town** ❷, a colourful recreational complex that includes quirky **Venus Fort** (www.venusfort.co.jp) mall, with a ceiling illuminated by an electronic sky that changes by the minute.

AROUND MIRAIKAN

Walk south then west past the blue arch of the Telecom Centre to the **National Museum of Emerging Science and Innovation** ❸ (tel: 3570 9151; www.miraikan.jst.go.jp; Wed–Mon 10am–5pm; charge), also known as the **Miraikan**, where you can learn about robot technology and other cutting-edge science projects.

Nearby soothe your limbs at the extraordinary **Oedo Onsen Monogatari** ❹ (tel: 5500 1126; www.ooedoonsen.jp; daily 11am–9am; charge) a traditional hot-spring bath with outdoor and indoor tubs, a sand bath, saunas and foot-massage baths.

A short walk northwest of the Miraikan is the **Museum of Maritime Science** ❺ (Fune-no-Kagakukan; tel: 5500 1111; www.funenokagakukan.or.jp; Tue–Sun 10am–5pm; charge). The building, designed in the shape of an ocean liner, has exhibitions tracing the development of shipping and sea transport. Docked outside and part of the museum are the decommissioned ferry *Yoteimaru* and *The Soya*, used for Japanese expeditions to the Antarctic.

ODAIBA BEACH

Walk to the northern edge of the island, where you will find an artificial **beach** and Daiba Station, to view the astonishing Kenzo Tange-designed **Fuji TV Building** ❻, consisting of two blocks connected by girder-like sky corridors and a 32m (100ft) diameter titanium-panelled sphere which replicates the structure of a wide-screen television set. The cathode-shaped globe contains both a restaurant and an **observatory** (Tue–Sun 10am–8pm; charge).

From the next monorail station – Odaiba-Kaihin-koen – you can access **Decks Tokyo Beach** ❼ (www.odaiba-decks.com), a shopping and amusement complex that includes the state-of-art arcade **Joypolis** (daily 10am–11.30pm; charge) and plenty of places to eat, including **Khazana**, see ⓘ①. More trendy shops and a multiplex cinema can be found next door at **Aqua City** (www.aquacity.jp).

RAINBOW BRIDGE

From Odaiba-Kaihin-koen Station a walkway leads up across the 918m (3,000ft) long **Rainbow Bridge** ❽. A pedestrian promenade links the two anchorages at each end of the suspension bridge. Crossing it takes about 30–40 minutes, but the views from the bridge are superb. From the observation gallery on the mainland side it is only a minute's walk to Shibaura-Futo, the stop for the monorail, which will take you back to Shimbashi Station.

Above from far left: Giant Sky Wheel at Palette Town; Oedo Onsen Monogatari.

Origin of Odaiba

The name Odaiba comes from the cannon emplacements placed in Tokyo Bay in 1853 to defend the city against any attack by Commodore Perry's Black Ships. The remains of two cannons can still be seen.

Food and Drink
① KHAZANA
5F Decks Tokyo Beach, 1-6-1 Daiba, Minato-ku; tel: 3599 6551; www.maharaja-group.com; daily 11am–11pm; station: Odaiba-Kaihin-koen; ¥¥
Khazana offers all-you-can-eat lunches (until 5pm) and good curries, plus outside tables with views of the Rainbow Bridge.

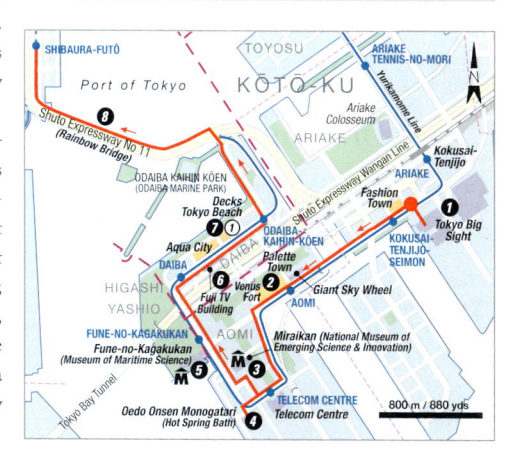

KAWAGOE

Less than a hour north of Tokyo, discover this 'Little Edo', famed for its historic core of kurazukuri – black-walled merchant houses, some dating from the 18th century – and the transported remains of Edo Castle.

Tourist Information
There's a tourist information office (tel: 049-222 5556; www.koedo.or.jp; daily 9am–4.30pm) at Kawagoe Station, where you can pick up a map of the town and an English pamphlet on the sights.

DISTANCE 40km (25 miles) north from Tokyo to Kawagoe; walking tour: 8km (5 miles)
TIME A full day
START/END Kawagoe Station
POINTS TO NOTE
Kawagoe is served by three train lines: JR, Seibu-Shinjuku and Tobu. The Tobu line express from Ikebukuro in Tokyo offers the fastest journey (30 min; ¥450), but the JR service only takes a few minutes longer and passes through Kawagoe Station, the start of this walk. Seibu-Shinjuku line trains (43 min from Shinjuku; ¥480) terminate at Hon-Kawagoe Station, about 1km (⅔ mile) closer to Kawagoe's historic core. Avoid Mondays, when several of the museums are closed.

Food and Drink
① KURAZUKURI HONPO
Ichiban-gai; daily 10am–5pm; ¥
Kawagoe is famous for edible creations made from *satsaimo* (sweet potato). You can try some at this confectionery shop and café.

Affectionately known as 'Little Edo', the old castle town of Kawagoe is a favourite of television directors looking for a ready-made set for historical dramas. The rivers that surround Kawagoe made it a strategic location on the way to the capital, and the town prospered as a supplier of goods to Edo (Tokyo) during the Tokugawa era (1603–1867). Now part of the Greater Tokyo area and a commuter suburb, it provides a glimpse of what most of the capital looked like before World War II and relentless modernisation both took their toll.

KUMANO-JINJA

From Kawagoe Station, it's a 15-minute walk to the town's historic core around Ichiban-gai. Follow the walkway on the left in front of the station to the Atre Department Store, walk down the steps and across the traffic lights to the Crea Mall, a busy pedestrian shopping street leading towards Ichiban-gai. At the first major intersection after about a 0.5km (⅓ mile), head one street to the left to reach Chuo-dori. On the right you will pass **Kumano-jinja** ❶, a small shrine housing one of the floats (called *dashi*) used in Kawagoe's lively annual festival.

AROUND ICHIBAN-GAI

A couple of short blocks later, you will know you have reached Ichiban-gai when you see the first *kurazukuri*, to the right. This impressive merchant building used to house the Kameya sweet shop and factory, and is now the **Yamazaki Museum of Art** ❷ (Fri–Wed 9.30am–5pm; charge), displaying screen paintings by the 19th-century artist Gaho Hashimoto. Entry includes a cup of tea and a traditional Japanese sweet *(okashi)*. Around the corner on Ichiban-gai is a functioning sweet shop and café, **Kurazukuri Honpo**, see ⓘ①.

Kurazukuri Shiryokan

As well as confectionery shops, Ichiban-gai is lined with other interesting stores, including ones that specialise in ceramics, knives, swords and woodwork items. Inside an old tobacco wholesaler you will find the **Kurazukuri Shiryokan** ❸ (tel: 049-222 5399; Tue–Sun 9am–5pm; charge). This is one of the first *kurazukuri* to be rebuilt after the great fire of 1893 that wiped out over a third of the city. The displays here give a good idea of what it used to be like to live in such houses.

Toki-no-Kane

Across the road from the Kurazukuri Shiryokan down a lane to the right is the **Toki-no-Kane** ❹, a three-storey wooden belltower that has become synonymous with Kawagoe. The tower was originally constructed in the 17th century and has since been through

Above from far left: *kurazukuri* rooftops; float embroidery at the Kawagoe Festival.

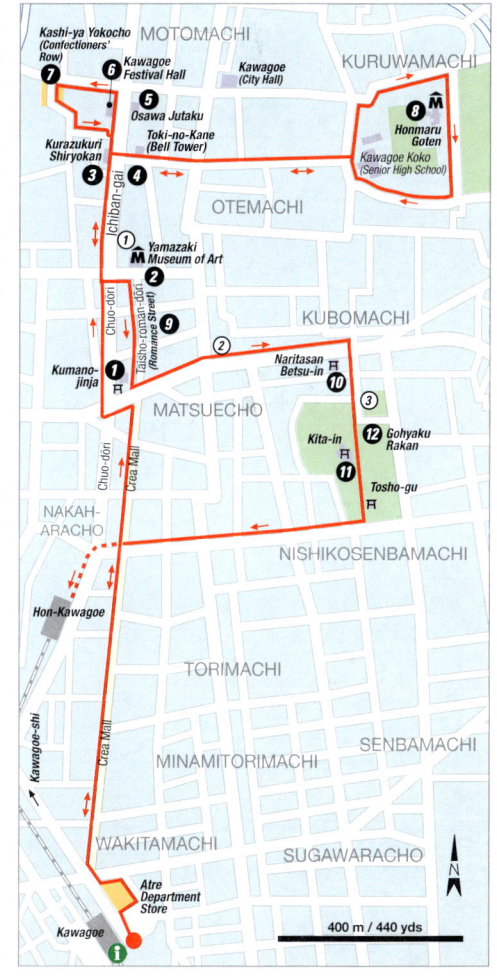

Above: statues at Gohyaku Rakan.

four editions, the most recent being this one dating from after the 1893 fire. Listen out for the bell, which tolls four times daily – at 6am, noon, 3pm and 6pm.

Osawa Jutaku

Further along the Ichiban-gai is the **Osawa Jutaku ❺**. Dating from 1792, it is Kawagoe's oldest *kurazukuri* and now a handicraft shop that sells traditional products like Japanese masks and dolls.

Kawagoe Festival Hall

Opposite is the **Kawagoe Festival Hall ❻** (tel: 049-225 2727; daily Apr–Sept 9am–6pm, Oct–Mar 9am–5pm, closed 2nd and 4th Wed of the month; charge), in which you can view two more of the ornate floats paraded around in the Kawagoe Festival, along with videos of past events.

Confectioners' Row

At the next main intersection after the Kawagoe Festival Hall turn left and walk a block to reach the narrow stone-paved lane on the left that is **Kashi-ya Yokocho ❼**, 'Confectioners' Row'. Souvenirs and trinkets have been added to the 22 nostalgically old-fashioned shops that sell traditional candies, crackers and other sweet treats such as purple sweet-potato ice cream.

REMAINS OF KAWAGOE CASTLE

Return to the belltower and walk east until you come to a school at the end of the street. You will need to loop round the school to find the one-time location of Kawagoe Castle. All that remains of the original fort is the entrance and main visitors' hall of the palace building, **Honmaru Goten ❽** (tel: 049-224 6015; Tue–Sun 9am–5pm; charge). Built by a local lord, Matsudaira Naritsune, in 1848, it's now a museum containing beautifully painted screens and waxwork dummies of samurai and lords of old.

TAISHO ROMANCE STREET

Retrace your route from Honmaru Goten back to the Yamazaki Art Museum. Running parallel to Chuo-dori one block to the east is **Taisho-roman-dori ❾**, meaning Taisho Romance Street. The handsome

---

Kawagoe Festival

Considered to be one of the Kanto area's top three festivals, Kawagoe's grand *matsuri*, held on the third Saturday and Sunday of October, attracts huge crowds. The tradition, which started back in the late 17th century, now sees some 25 extravagantly decorated floats, each representing a different area of the city and attended by costumed teams, parade through the streets around Ichiban-gai. The highlight of the festival is the Hikkawase – the Pulling of the Floats – when passing teams square off against each other in a cacophonous performance of music and chanting.

stone façades of the shops here date from the Taisho era (1912–26) and contrast nicely with those of the nearby *kurazukuri*. Before the street leads back into the Crea Mall turn left and walk east for one block to find the grilled-eel restaurant **Ichinoya**, see ②.

Naritasan Betsu-in

A short walk east of Ichinoya is the temple **Naritasan Betsu-in** ⑩. On the 28th of each month a flea market is hosted in its grounds.

KITA-IN

Immediately after the temple turn right and head a few blocks south, past the noodle restaurant **Kotobukian**, see ③, to reach **Kita-in** ⑪ (www.kawagoe.com/kitain; daily 9am–4.30pm; charge), an important Buddhist temple-museum that dates back to 830. It has been destroyed several times by fire, but after one conflagration in 1638, the third shogun, Tokugawa Iemitsu, ordered that parts of the original Edo Castle (situated where the Imperial Palace now stands) be transported here to aid in the reconstruction. From these historic wooden buildings – the likes of which do not now exist in Tokyo itself – you can admire a traditional Japanese garden planted with plum, cherry and maple trees as well as hydrangea and azaleas.

Gohyaku Rakan

Apart from the Edo Castle remains, Kita-in's other crowd-pleaser is the **Gohyaku Rakan** ⑫ grove of stone statues carved between 1782 and 1825. Meaning '500 statues', there are actually 540 depictions of the disciples of the Buddha, no two alike. One figure scratches his head, a couple get drunk on wine, others meditate, rub a sore foot or beat drums. One old sage is shown holding a teapot and cup.

While at the temple you can also admire a mini-version of Nikko's **Tosho-gu** *(see p.92)*, built to honour Tokugawa Ieyasu, the first shogun.

Heading Back

Exit the temple to the south, turn right and walk around 1km (²⁄₃ mile) back towards Crea Mall and either the Hon-Kawagoe or Kawagoe Station to return to Tokyo.

Kurazukuri

Kawagoe is best known for its collection of around 30 *kurazukuri* – merchant houses built in the same style as the neighbouring fire-resistant storehouses, with thick mortar walls, double-door shutters on the upper windows and elaborately tiled *onigawara*-style roofs. During the Edo period the walls of these buildings were covered with charcoal powder mixed with plaster and buffed to a mirror-like shine. It is said that women in Kawagoe used to adjust their kimono and hair while gazing at their reflections in the shiny black surfaces.

Food and Drink

② ICHINOYA
1-18-10 Matsue-cho; tel: 049-222 0354; daily 11.30am–9pm; ¥¥

The delicacy *unagi* (grilled eel) is served at this popular two-floor restaurant. Sit on *tatami* mats and enjoy a set lunch of the savoury-sweet fish with rice.

③ KOTOBUKIAN
1-2-11 Kosemba-cho; tel: 049-225 1184; Mon–Tue and Thur–Fri 11.30am–5pm, Sat–Sun 11.30am–8pm; ¥¥

Located beside Kita-in, this restaurant specialises in *wariko-soba* – green-tea buckwheat noodles served in lacquered bento boxes with a variety of other dishes.

KAMAKURA & ENOSHIMA

Spend the day at the seaside discovering the venerable Zen temples and shrines of Japan's ancient capital, Kamakura. Come face to face with the Daibutsu (Great Buddha), then visit the sacred island of Enoshima.

Tourist Information
At Kamakura Station there is a tourist information office (tel: 0467-223 350; www.kcn-net.org/kamakura; daily 9am–5pm) where the staff speak English. Free maps are available, and they can tell you where to rent a bike should you wish to pedal around the area.

Below: Tokei-ji.

DISTANCE 45km (28 miles) from Toyko to Kamakura; tour: 11.5km (7¼ miles)
TIME A full day
START Kita-Kamakura Station
END Enoshima Station
POINTS TO NOTE
Either take a JR Yokosuka line train from Tokyo Station or a JR Shonan-Shinjuku line train from Shinjuku or Shibuya. Make sure the train is bound for Yokosuka or Kurihama, otherwise you will have to change at Ofuna. It's worth investing in the Kamakura-Enoshima Free Kippu (¥1,970), a two-day discount ticket covering the return trip by JR trains from Tokyo, plus unlimited travel on the Enoden line (www.enoden.co.jp) and Shonan monorail connecting Enoshima with Ofuna.

Wedged between wooded hills and the sea, just one hour south by train from central Tokyo, Kamakura is saturated in history. With a proliferation of temples and shrines, the town served between 1192 and 1333 as the shogun's capital. If you are only visiting for the day, it's best to stick to a few carefully selected highlights and leave some time to enjoy the beaches and ocean vistas around neighbouring Enoshima.

KAMAKURA

A cluster of temples just two minutes' walk from Kita-Kamakura Station is the ideal place to begin. Surrounded by ancient cedars, **Engaku-ji** ❶ (tel: 0467-220 478; daily Apr–Oct 8am–5pm, Nov–Mar 8am–4pm; charge), a major Zen temple founded in 1282 to honour soldiers killed during Kublai Khan's failed invasion of the country, is the closest. Laid out according to Chinese Zen principles, the main buildings and numerous sub-temples evoke an austere beauty, softened by foliage, shrubbery and a pond. The Chinese-style Shariden, one of the finest buildings here, is said to contain a tooth of the Buddha.

Tokei-ji

Continue southeast along the main road until you reach **Tokei-ji** ❷ (tel: 0467-

221 663; www.tokeiji.com; daily Mar–Oct 8.30am–5pm, Nov–Feb 8.30am–4pm; charge), a 13th-century Buddhist temple that originally served as a nunnery. Also known as the 'Divorce Temple', this was one of the few places where women could escape from abusive husbands. Until the mid-19th century, a man was only required to send his wife a letter as notice of divorce, a right that was not reciprocal. If a woman could reach Tokei-ji and remain there for three years, her husband would be summoned and obliged to sign papers annulling the marriage. Several of these documents are on display in the temple's Treasure House. Stroll through the flower-filled gardens to the temple's rear where, in a modest cemetery, lie the remains of the nuns buried beneath neglected and mossy headstones.

Kencho-ji

Follow the main Kamakura-kaido road across the railway tracks until you reach the grand entrance gate to **Kencho-ji** ❸ (tel: 0467-220 981; daily 8.30am–4.30pm; charge). Founded in 1253, it is one of Japan's oldest Zen training temples. A grove of ancient juniper trees almost conceals the main Butsu-den (Buddha Hall), a rather misleading term as the main image here is of the bodhisattva Jizo, floating on a bed of lotuses. Hojo, the abbot's quarters, the last and finest wooden structure at Kencho-ji, is backed by an exquisite garden, designed by the priest Muso Kokushi.

Remove your shoes and walk along a balcony of smooth, time-worn wood to reach the garden. On leaving, you will pass the vegetarian restaurant **Hachi-no-ki**, see ❶, on the main road.

Above from far left: red-painted hall at the shrine Tsurugaoka Hachiman-gu; tranquil scene at Engaku-ji; incense burner.

Food and Drink
① **HACHI-NO-KI**

7 Yamanouchi, Kamakura; tel: 0120-228 719; www.hachinoki.co.jp; Tue–Fri 11am–2pm, Sat–Sun 11am–3pm; ¥¥
Next to Kencho-ji, this is the main branch of a famous restaurant serving the delicate Buddhist vegetarian cuisine known as *shojin ryori*. If it's full, there's another branch closer to Kita-Kamakura Station.

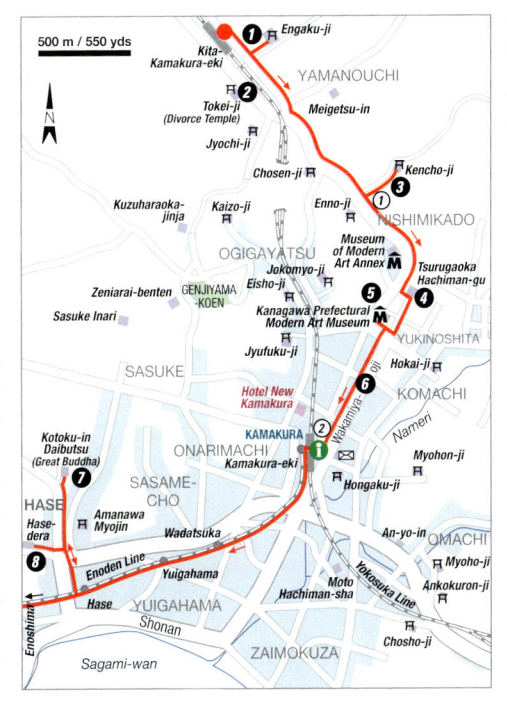

Place to Stay

If you wish to make this more than a day trip, one of the most atmospheric places to stay is Hotel New Kamakura (13-2 Onarimachi, Kamakura; tel: 0467-222 230; www.newkamakura.com), in a historic building offering both simple Western and Japanese-style rooms. It's less than a minute's walk north from the western side of Kamakura Station.

Tsurugaoka Hachiman-gu

Continue downhill towards the centre of Kamakura until you reach the rear entrance to the shrine **Tsurugaoka Hachiman-gu** ❹, marked by a series of red-painted *torii* (entrance gates). Since the 11th century this has been the guardian shrine for the Minamoto clan, founders of the Kamakura shogunate. Most of the buildings are reconstructions, but the red-painted halls, souvenir stalls and flow of visitors make it one of the city's most colourful pilgrimage spots. A large gingko tree on the left of the steps up to the shrine marks the spot where the third shogun was assassinated by a jealous nephew in 1219.

Kanagawa Prefectural Museum of Modern Art

Within the shrine precincts you will also find the **Kanagawa Prefectural Museum of Modern Art** ❺ (tel: 0467-225 000; www.moma.pref.kanagawa.jp; Tue–Sun 9.30am–5pm; charge), which has regular exhibitions of Japanese and foreign artists. The museum's annexe is back on the main road before Tsurugaoka Hachiman-gu.

Wakamiya-oji

Cross the Drum Bridge and exit the shrine onto **Wakamiya-oji** ❻. This boulevard, with its central reservation planted with cherry trees and azaleas, is a popular flower-viewing site in spring. Walk until you reach the mock *torii* gate at the end of the central reservation, and turn right to find **Nakamura-an**, see ①②, one of Kamakura's most famous noodle restaurants. From here it is less than a minute's walk west to Kamakura Station.

HASE

To reach the next sight, you will need to use the Enoden line train which connects Kamakura and Enoshima. Board the train at Kamakura Station and alight three stops later at **Hase**. From here it's just a few minutes' walk north along the main street to the entrance of **Kotoku-in** ❼ (daily Apr–Sept 7am–

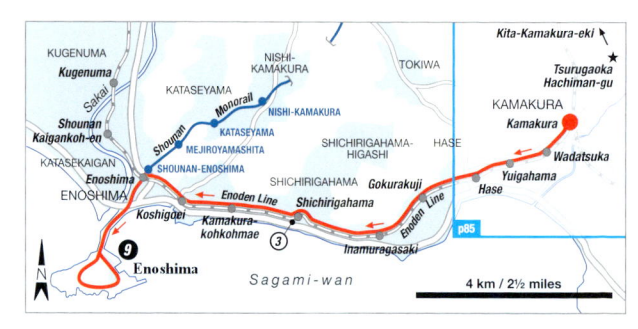

6pm, Oct–Mar 7am–5.30pm; charge), which houses the *Daibutsu* – the Great Buddha *(see feature)*. For a small charge, you can climb inside this giant hollow bronze statue.

Hase-dera

Return in the direction of Hase Station, turn right and enter the grounds of the 8th-century temple **Hase-dera** ❽ (tel: 0467-226 300; www.hasedera.jp; daily Mar–Sept 8am–5pm, Oct–Feb 8am–4.30pm; charge). Walk past an ornamental pond and up a flight of steps to reach the main temple precincts, which have fine views of Kamakura Bay. The temple is renowned for its eleven-faced Kannon, made from a single camphor and covered in gold leaf. At 9.3m (30ft) high, it is Japan's tallest wooden statue.

ENOSHIMA

Board the Enoden train again and get off at Enoshima Station. It's a 15-minute walk from here and across the 600m/yd causeway to the tiny sacred island of **Enoshima** ❾, its hilly slopes plastered with an extraordinary collection of shrines, grottoes and souvenir shops. Local fishermen traditionally came to Enoshima to pray for a bountiful catch. Escalators take the faithful to higher reaches, but it's not difficult to follow the old pilgrim routes as they wind up through this island of the gods.

Apart from its shrines and sacred caves, the island boasts a yachting harbour, a botanical garden (charge) containing more than 300 species of tropical plants, and several cafés with fine views of Mount Fuji.

If you would like to enjoy a meal or cocktail before leaving the seaside, though, a recommended spot to do so is the less touristy restaurant and bar **bills**, see ①③, steps away from Shichirigahama Station on the Enoden line, a few stops back towards Kamakura.

Above from far left: the Great Buddha; view of Mount Fuji and Enoshima.

The Great Buddha

Survivor of fires, typhoons and multiple earthquakes, the 11m (35ft) image of Amida Nyorai, the Buddha who receives souls into the Western Paradise, is Japan's second-largest bronze statue. Cast in 1252, it was originally housed in a wooden hall that suffered a series of catastrophes, culminating in a great tidal wave that swept the building away in 1495. These disasters were interpreted as a sign that the Buddha wished to remain outside, and the statue, exposed to the sun and salt-winds ever since, is now an oxidised, streaked green.

Food and Drink

② NAKAMURA-AN

1-7-6 Komachi, Kamakura; tel: 0467-253 500; Fri–Wed 11.30am–6pm; ¥

There's almost always a queue in this rustic *soba* restaurant, where the buckwheat noodles are handmade and cheap.

③ BILLS

Weekend House Alley 2F, 1-1-1 Shichirigahama, Kamakura; tel: 0467-331 778; www.bills-jp.net; Sun–Thur 9am–10pm, Mon until 5pm, Fri–Sat until 11pm; ¥¥

Sydney-based chef Bill Granger brings his famous scrambled eggs and laid-back brand of cuisine to this sunny, sophisticated spot overlooking Shichirigahama Beach.

HAKONE

This excursion, covering the hot-spring and lakeside resort of Hakone, takes in a range of museums, historical sights, Japan's oldest European-style hotel and – if the weather plays ball – postcard views of Mount Fuji.

Places to Stay

Apart from the Fujiya Hotel, Hakone has many other excellent places to stay, including a few top-class *ryokan*. One of the most exclusive and expensive is Gora Kadan (tel: 0460-823 333; www.gorakadan. com) in Gora, where you will also find the stylishly designed Hyatt Regency Hakone Resort & Spa (tel: 0460-822 000; www.hakone.regency. hyatt.com). Budget travellers can bunk down at the Hakone Lake Villa Youth Hostel (tel: 0460-831 610; www.jyh.or.jp) in Moto-Hakone overlooking Lake Ashino.

DISTANCE 90km (56 miles) southwest from Tokyo to Hakone; tour: 26km (16 miles)
TIME 1 or 2 days
START/END Hakone-Yumoto Station
POINTS TO NOTE
At a brisk clip, you can cover this itinerary in a day. Whether you do this or spend a couple of days here, save money with the three-day Hakone Pass (¥5,500) or the two-day Hakone Winter Weekday Pass (¥4700, available Dec–mid-Mar Mon–Thur), both of which cover a return trip on the Odakyu line from Shinjuku to Odawara, plus unlimited use of the Hakone Tozan Railway, Sounzan funicular, Hakone Ropeway, boats on Lake Ashino and most local buses. They also get you discounts at many of Hakone's attractions. For ¥870 extra, ride the Odakyu line's 'Romance Car', a direct express train from Shinjuku Station to Hakone-Yumoto. For more details, see www.odakyu.jp. If possible, visit Hakone on a weekday, when it is quieter.

Stressed out Tokyoites flock to Hakone to relax in the local *onsen* – hot-spring baths – and enjoy the scenic surroundings. Join the fun of touring the region on multiple forms of transport, including a cable car across a steaming volcanic field and a mock-17th-century galleon over a lovely lake with Mount Fuji in the background.

HAKONE-YUMOTO

The circular route begins at **Hakone-Yumoto** ❶, a tourist town jam-packed with souvenir shops and resort hotels. Its saving grace is its excellent *onsen*, the most convenient of which is the small **Kappa Tengoku Notemburo** (777 Yumoto; tel: 0460-856 121; daily 10am–10pm; charge), a short walk uphill from the train station, offering outdoor baths (called *rotemburo*).

HAKONE TOZAN RAILWAY

Connect to the **Hakone Tozan Railway** ❷ at Hakone-Yumoto Station. The line, which has the feeling of a delightfully slow trolley car, has several switchbacks to cope with the mountain slopes. As the train negotiates the inclines, the carriages virtually brush the camellias, azaleas, hydrangeas and other flowering shrubs and bushes that grow beside the track or on the borders of dense wooded areas along the way.

FUJIYA HOTEL

Alight at Miyanoshita Station. This village and hot-spring resort is located along a ravine; it is just a short walk from the station to the historic **Fujiya Hotel** ❸ (tel: 0460-822 211; www.fujiya-hotel.co.jp), dating from 1878 when it was Japan's first European-style hotel. With its 1930s wood-panelled dining room, a library full of old books, and waitresses in Agatha Christie-period uniforms, it remains a charming place. Whether or not you stay, it's worth eating at the **Orchid Lounge**, see ⑪①.

HAKONE OPEN-AIR MUSEUM

Return to the Tozan line and continue for another two stops until you arrive at Chokoku-no-Mori, the station for the **Hakone Open-Air Museum** ❹ (tel: 0460-821 161; www.hakone-oam.or.jp; Mar–Nov 9am–5pm, Dec–Feb 9am–4pm; charge). It features modern sculptures by the likes of

> ## Food and Drink
> ### ① ORCHID LOUNGE
> Fujiya Hotel, Miyanoshita; ¥¥
> Afternoon tea at the Fujiya is a cherished ritual, but there's nothing to stop you pausing for morning coffee either. At both times yummy baked goods from the hotel's Picot Bakery are served.

Above from far left: Hakone Tozan Railway; one of Hakone-Yumoto's outdoor baths.

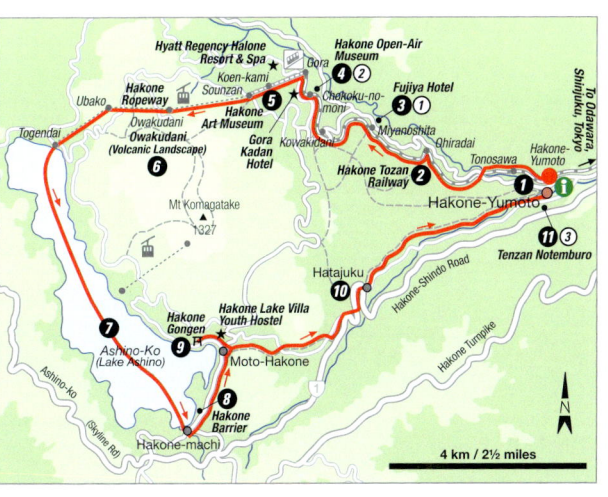

Tourist Information
The Odakyu Sightseeing Service Centre (daily 8am–6pm) at the west exit of Shinjuku Station has English-speaking staff who can advise about visiting Hakone. In Hakone-Yumoto, across the road from the bus terminal and close to the train station is the helpful Hakone Tourist Information Office (tel: 0460-855 700; www.hakone.or.jp daily; Apr–Nov 9.30am–6pm, Dec–Mar 9am–5.30pm).

HAKONE OPEN-AIR MUSEUM 89

Above from left: tourist town of Hakone-Yumoto; galleon on Lake Ashino and the Hakone Gongen's red *torri*.

Calder, Brancusi, Rodin, Giacometti, Henry Moore and other Western masters, artfully placed in landscaped gardens that afford superb views of sea and mountains. The Picasso Pavilion contains sculptures, paintings, ceramics and tiles, as well as galleries devoted to Renoir, Chagall, Miró and Japanese artists, such as Hayashi Takeshi and Umehara Ryuzaburo. There are several places to eat at the museum, including the restaurant **Bella Foresta**, see ②.

HAKONE ART MUSEUM

The terminus of the Tozan line is only one stop away from the museum at **Gora**. Here, transfer to a **funicular tram** for the 10-minute journey to Sounzan, the starting point for the cable car that crosses Mount Soun.

Before that, though, get off at Koen-kami Station on the funicular to visit the **Hakone Art Museum** ❺ (tel: 0460-822 623; Fri–Wed 9.30am–4.30pm; charge), which specialises in Japanese ceramics and tea-ceremony utensils. Some outstanding examples of Bizen pottery and ancient ceramics are on display, and outside there is a lovely mossy garden with a bamboo grove, maple trees and a teahouse.

OWAKUDANI

Travel on to **Sounzan**, catching the cable car called the **Hakone Ropeway** for a giddy 30-minute journey over the mountains to Lake Ashino. If the weather is clear (it often isn't, particularly during the summer months), you will be able to get a good view of Mount Fuji (Fuji-san) during the journey.

Be sure to get off at the first stop, **Owakudani** ❻ ('great boiling hell'), a bleached terrain so barren-looking you could be forgiven for thinking you had been put down on a dead planet. Hakone has a history of volcanic eruptions, and the stench of sulphur and clouds of steam from the fumaroles at Owakudani are a constant reminder of how unstable the ground beneath you is. Locals boil eggs in the sulphur pits and then sell them to visitors with the unlikely assurance that by eating one your life will be extended by seven years.

Food and Drink

② BELLA FORESTA
Hakone Open-Air Museum, Ninotaira, Hakone-machi; ¥¥
The museum's buffet restaurant offers a wide range of Japanese and Western dishes, but if none of them suit there's the dim-sum restaurant Hakone Yamucharow, serving Hong Kong-style dumplings, and two cafés – one designed as a homage to Picasso, the other in the style of a British pub.

③ TENZAN NOTEMBURO
208 Yumoto-Chaya, Hakone-Yumoto; ¥¥
The *onsen* complex is also an excellent place to eat after taking a bath. Its three restaurants serve *shabu shabu* (sautéed beef) and *teppanyaki* (grilled meat dishes), as well as humble bowls of noodles.

AROUND LAKE ASHINO

The cable car terminates at **Togendai**, at the northern end of **Lake Ashino** ❼ (Ashino-ko) where, for the next stage of your journey, you should board one of the colourful mock-galleons that ply between here and Hakone-Machi. The boats are outrageously kitsch, but the journey across this serene lake is magical.

Hakone Barrier

You will disembark from the boat at **Hakone-machi**, which is the site of the **Hakone Barrier** ❽ (Hakone Sekisho; daily 9am–4.30pm; charge), a replica of the original checkpoint that stood here during the Edo period. The barrier marks an important point on the Tokaido Road that ran between Kyoto and Edo (Tokyo). An exhibition hall beside the barrier provides the historical background to the road. A 1km ($^2/_3$-mile) section of the original Tokaido makes for a pleasant walk from the barrier, under tall cryptomeria trees, to the lakeside village of Moto-Hakone.

Hakone Gongen

As you approach **Moto-Hakone**, you will get a lovely view of a red *torii* gate, which stands in the water and is framed by forest as well as, if you are lucky, the glorious backdrop of Mount Fuji. The gate is part of the shrine known as **Hakone Gongen** ❾. Hidden among trees close to the shore, the shrine was founded in 757 and was once a popular place for samurai to pray.

HATAJUKU

Buses run from Moto-Hakone back to Hakone-Yumoto for the return journey to Tokyo. Alternatively, you can make the 11km (7-mile) hike through the forests, tracing the route of the Tokaido via the village of **Hatajuku** ❿, which is famous for its woodwork craftsmen who specialise in marquetry.

Along the way you can pause, just as pilgrims of old did, at the still functioning **Amazake-jaya Teahouse**, where you can sample *amazake*, which is a sweet and mildly alcoholic milky rice drink.

TENZAN NOTEMBURO

About 2km ($1^1/_4$ miles) from Hakone-Yumoto, the Tokaido hiking path passes the luxurious *onsen* complex **Tenzan Notemburo** ⓫ (tel: 0460-864 126; daily 9am–11pm; charge). The bathing here is segregated, with indoor and outdoor pools designed in attractive arrangements of wood and rock. Men also have access to a clay sauna hut. You can dine here as well, see ③, before walking or catching the complimentary shuttle bus back to Hakone-Yumoto Station.

Below: sculptures at the Hakone Open Air Museum.

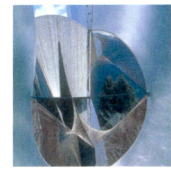

NIKKO

Set off early for a full day's exploration of the opulent shrines and mausoleums of the early shoguns in the verdant hills of Nikko. Pack an overnight bag if you also wish to visit nearby Lake Chuzenji.

Entry Charges
The ¥1,000 *nisha-ichiji* combination ticket sold at booths outside Rinno-ji's Sanbutsu-do and Tosho-gu's Omote-mon will save you some money. It covers entry to Rinno-ji, Futarasan Shrine and most of Tosho-gu. Add ¥520 if you wish to tag on entry to see Tosho-gu's sleeping cat carving and Ieyasu's Mausoleum.

Tourist Information
There's an information desk (tel: 0288-534 511; daily 8.30am–5pm) in Tobu Nikko Station, while the main tourist office (tel: 0288-542 496; www.nikko-jp.org; daily 8.30am–5pm) is midway along the main road from the station to Tosho-gu.

> **DISTANCE** 128km (80 miles) north from Tokyo to Nikko; walking tour: 3.5km (2¼ miles)
> **TIME** 1 or 2 days
> **START/END** Shin-kyo Bridge
> **POINTS TO NOTE**
> Although Nikko is accessible by JR trains, most people come here on the Tobu-Nikko line from Asakusa in Tokyo; in Nikko the JR and Tobu stations are beside each other. Tobu's Spacia limited express takes 1 hour 55 min, the cheaper *kyuko* service an extra 15 min. If you opt for the latter, be sure to sit in one of the first two carriages, as some of the trains divide at Shimo Imaichi Station, the stop before Nikko.
>
> If you are planning to include a visit to Lake Chuzenji, buy the All Nikko Pass (¥4,400); for details about the pass and train times, see www.tobu.co.jp/foreign.
>
> In Nikko frequent local buses from the train stations allow you to skip the 20-minute walk up the town's somewhat shabby high street towards the shrine complex.

An *onsen* (hot-spring) resort in the mountains of Tochigi Prefecture, Nikko is best known as the location of the Tosho-gu shrine and mausoleum.

TOSHO-GU

The shrine **Tosho-gu** was built to honour Tokugawa Ieyasu, the shogun who unified Japan around 1600 and founded a political dynasty that lasted for over 250 years. Some 1,500 craftsmen and artists were brought to Nikko for a period of two years by Tokugawa Iemitsu, Ieyasu's grandson and the third shogun. The shrine was completed in 1634 to a mixed reception. Some considered it to be a fitting tribute to Japan's greatest shogun; others regarded it as a gaudy extravagance, more expressive of Chinese Tang-dynasty tastes and too much of a deviation from the simple, understated design of most Shinto shrines. Regardless, the complex received Unesco World Heritage Status in 2004 and is always inundated with visitors.

Shin-kyo Bridge
Marking the entrance to Tosho-gu's grounds is the vermilion-painted

Shin-kyo ❶ (Sacred Bridge; 9am–4pm; charge) over the Daiya River. In former times, only the shogun and imperial messengers were allowed to cross the wooden bridge, which is best viewed from the road rather than close up.

Rinno-ji

Cross the road from the bridge and follow the steps of a path that winds up to a **statue of Shodo Shonin**, the priest who founded Nikko more than 1,200 years ago when the mountains in this area were honoured as gods. Close by is the site of **Rinno-ji** ❷ (daily Apr–Oct 8am–4.30pm, Nov–Mar 8am–3.30pm; charge), a temple which Shodo founded in 766. The temple's main hall, the **Sanbutsu-do**, enshrines three huge wood-carved and gilded statues: a thousand-armed Kannon, the Amida Buddha and a horse-headed Kannon. A separate ticket gains you entrance to Rinno-ji's **Treasure House** and **Shoyo-en**, a classic, landscaped stroll garden that was completed in 1815.

Main Entrance

Exit Rinno-ji onto broad Omote-sando, the main approach to Tosho-gu's original stone *torii* gate. A five-storey pagoda stands to the left, an example of how Buddhism and Shinto are blended here. Ascend another set of stone steps and pass through **Omote-mon**, Tosho-gu's

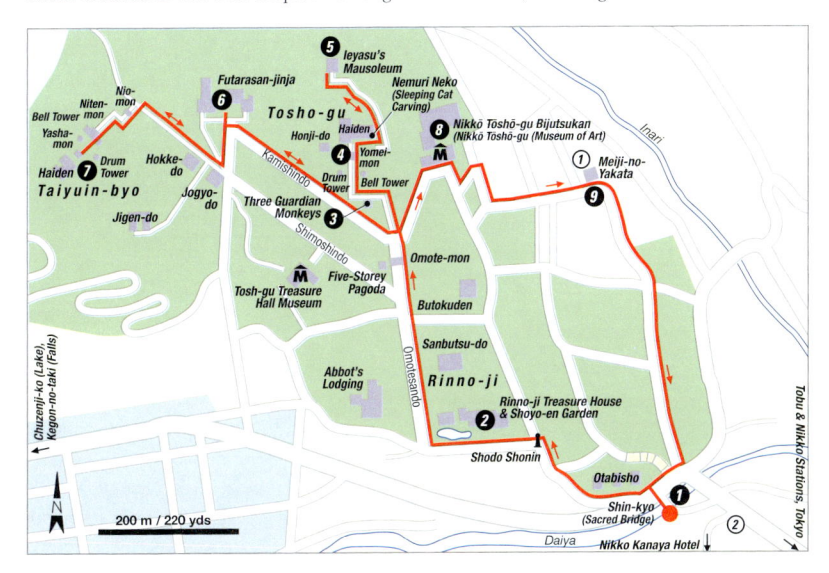

Above from far left: Shin-kyo, the Sacred Bridge that marks the entrance to Tosho-gu; the rich colours of autumnal leaves draw visitors to Nikko; dragon at Rinno-ji.

Above from left:
Three Guardian Monkeys; Lake Chuzenji to the west of Nikko.

entrance gate (daily Apr–Oct 8am–4.30pm, Nov–Mar 8am–3.30pm; charge), to reach the area containing the sacred storehouses and stable, and the carving of **Three Guardian Monkeys** ❸ in their famous pose, 'See no evil, hear no evil, speak no evil'. The next terrace contains stone lanterns donated by *daimyo* (feudal lords) from all over Japan. A large revolving bronze lantern, with the Tokugawa family crest mistakenly engraved upside down, is a gift from Holland, the only country in the 17th century allowed limited diplomatic and trade relations with Japan.

Yomei-mon

The lavish gate **Yomei-mon** ❹ stands at the top of a short flight of steps to the upper terrace. Carved and gilded with more than 400 images of flowers, dragons, birds and Chinese sages, it is also known as the Twilight Gate because of the risk that you will become so mesmerised by it that you will spend the whole day there. To the gate's left, behind a drum tower, there's the **Honji-do**, famous for its huge 'roaring dragon' ceiling painting. If you stand under its head and clap, you will hear the dragon roar.

Ieyasu's Mausoleum

Having passed through the Yomei-mon, most visitors turn right and continue up to Ieyasu's Mausoleum. As you leave the shrine, look out for a small carving on the lintel. This is the sleeping cat *(nemuri neko)* carving, which has become Nikko's mascot.

In contrast to the flamboyance of the shrine, there is a more sacred air to **Ieyasu's Mausoleum** ❺ (charge), surrounded by cryptomeria trees and reached by 200 steps.

Food and Drink

① GYOUSHIN-TEI
2339-1 Sannai; tel: 0288-533 751; daily noon–8pm; ¥¥¥
Behind the Western-style restaurant Meiji-no-Yakata is this traditional place where you sit on *tatami* mats and gaze at a lovely garden while eating a *shojin-ryori* vegetarian banquet.

② HIPPARI DAKO
1011 Kami-hatsuishicho; tel: 0288-532 933; daily 11am–7pm; ¥
On the main road up to the Shin-kyo Bridge is this eternally popular café, serving noodles and *yakitori* (skewers of grilled chicken) and plastered with the business cards of thousands of visitors.

Lake Chuzenji

A visit to Lake Chuzenji (Chuzenji-ko) and the spectacular Kegon Falls (Kegon-no-taki), located 10km (6 miles) west of Nikko, is highly recommended. The lake is reached via the Iroha Slope, a road with scenic views from a series of hairpin bends, each one named after a different phonetic character in the Japanese alphabet. Both Chuzenji village and the tiny hot-spring resort of Yumoto, located on a plateau surrounded by mountains a short distance from Lake Chuzenji, offer plenty of accommodation should you wish to stay here and enjoy the spectacular scenery and natural surroundings. The bus ride up to Lake Chuzenji from Nikko takes 50 minutes. However, in autumn the journey can take up to three times longer.

FUTARASAN-JINJA

Retrace your route to the exit of Tosho-gu, bear right at the pagoda and walk along a path lined with stone lanterns to reach the grounds of **Futarasan-jinja** ❻. Dedicated to nearby Mount Nantai, the simplicity of this red, lacquered shrine and its pleasant garden is a welcome relief after the highly accomplished but ostentatious shrine of Tosho-gu. You can enjoy a bowl of *macha* here, the frothy green brew made during the tea ceremony. The grounds of the shrine contain a famous bronze *bakemono toro* (phantom lantern), cast in 1292. According to legend, the lantern used to roam the shrine precincts at night, terrorising its night watchmen.

TAIYUIN-BYO

Just beyond the Futarasan Shrine is the attractive **Taiyuin-byo** ❼ (daily Apr–Oct 8am–4.30pm, Nov–Mar 8am–3.30pm; charge), the mausoleum of Tokugawa Iemitsu. It's intentionally less ostentatious than Tosho-gu and usually a lot less crowded.

NIKKO TOSHO-GU MUSEUM OF ART

From Taiyuin-byo return to Omotemon and, facing away from Tosho-gu, take the left path leading to the **Nikko Tosho-gu Museum of Art** ❽ (Nikko Tosho-gu Bijutsukan; Apr–Oct 8am–5pm, Nov–Mar 8am–4pm; charge). The collection of painted screens and sliding doors, housed in a wooden building erected in 1928, is one of the finest exhibitions of its kind in Japan.

MEIJI-NO-YAKATA

Next to the museum are the grounds of **Meiji-no-Yakata** ❾, an early 20th-century Western-style holiday villa. It now houses several restaurants including, to the rear of the main building, the vegetarian **Gyoushin-tei**, see ①. Alternatively, it's a short walk back to the Shin-kyo Bridge and main road, along which you will find both the Nikko Kanaya Hotel and the simple eatery **Hippari Dako**, see ②.

Places to Stay

Founded in 1873, the venerable Nikko Kanaya Hotel (1300 Kami-Hatsuishi-machi, Nikko; tel: 0288-540 001; www.kanaya hotel.co.jp) has long been the abode of choice for visitors to Nikko. The same company operates the luxurious and more modern Chuzenji Kanaya Hotel (tel: 0288-510 001) overlooking Lake Chuzenji and 2km (1¼ miles) away from the tourist village. Both hotels have good restaurants and cafés.

Below: Yomei-mon.

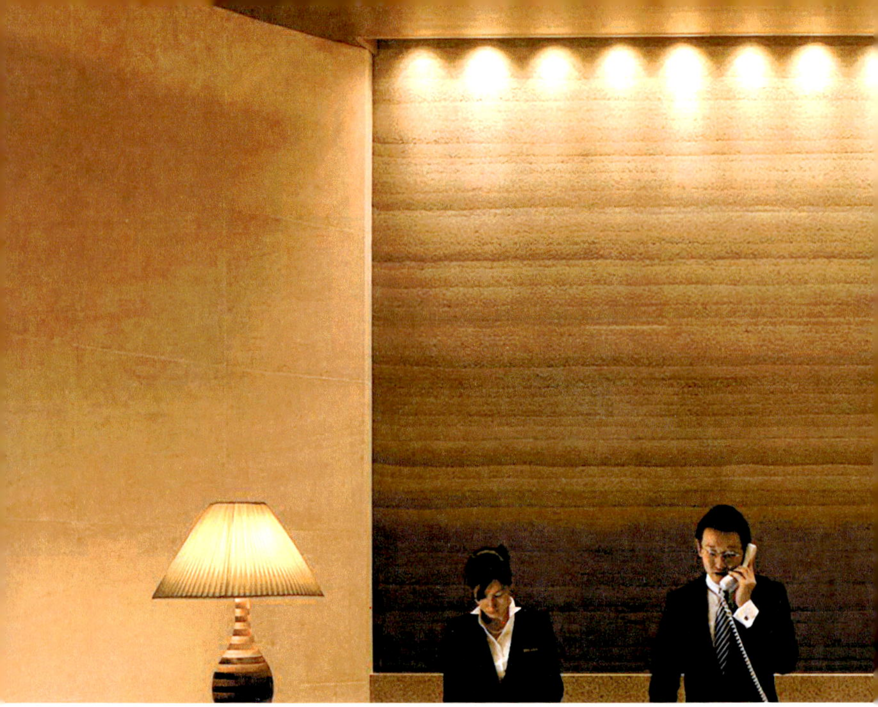
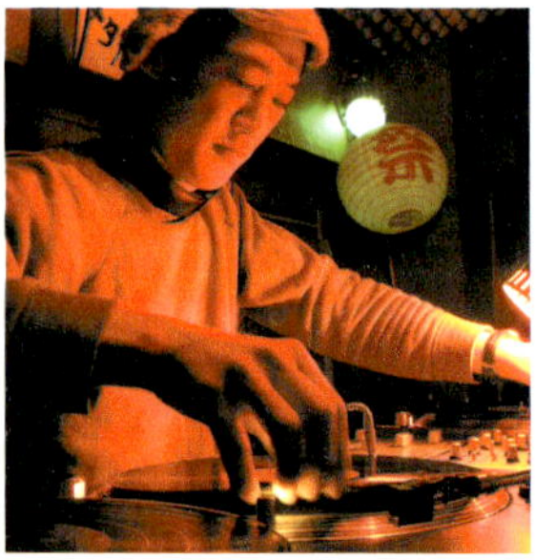
祭
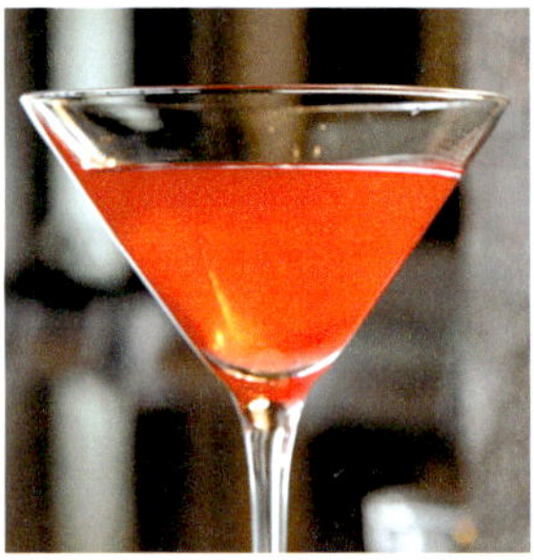
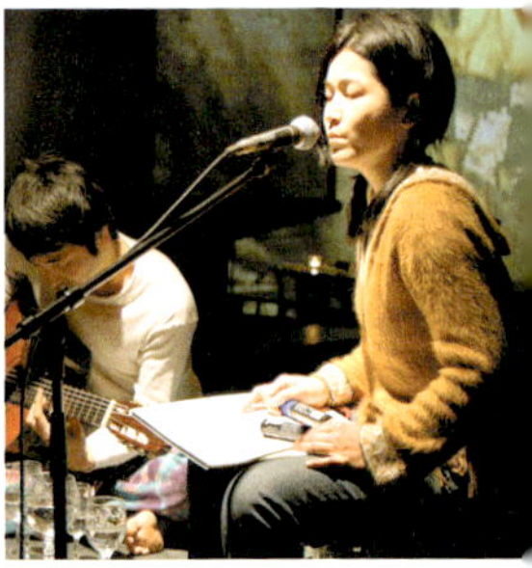
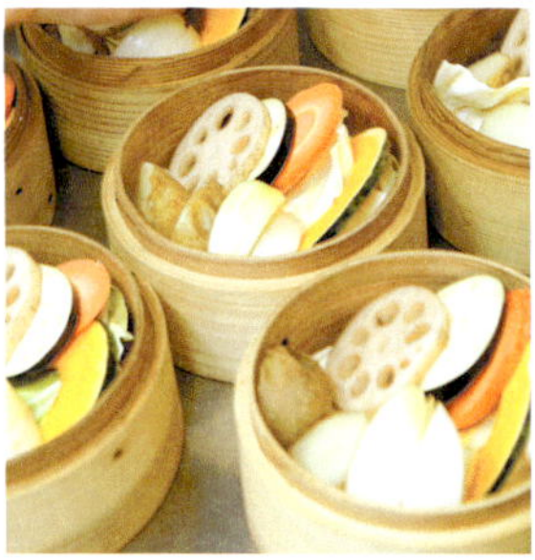
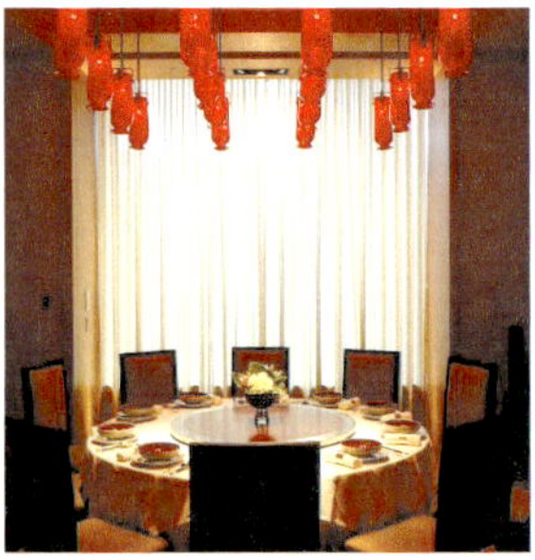
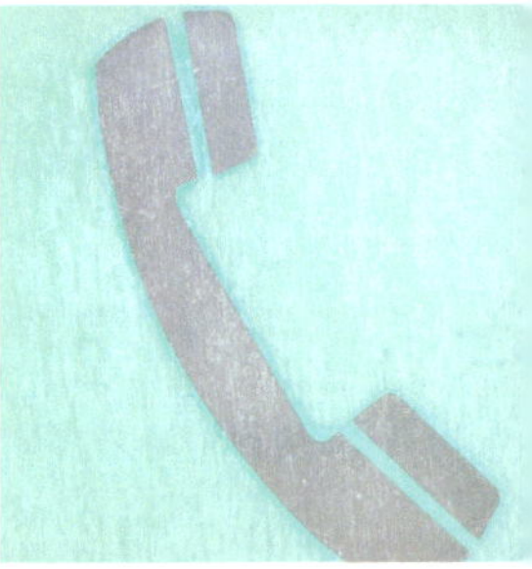
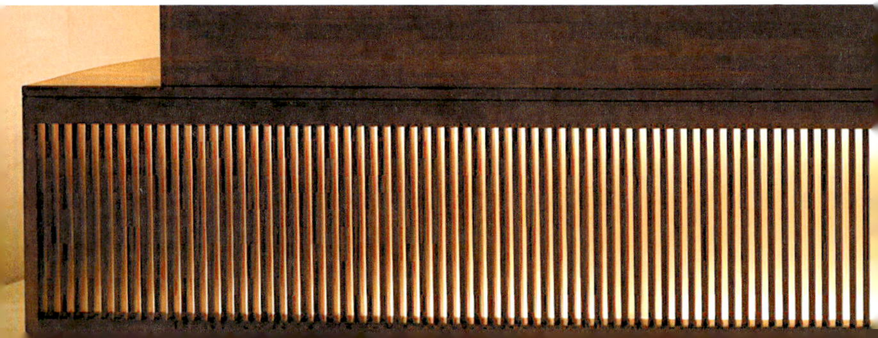

DIRECTORY

A user-friendly alphabetical listing of practical information, plus hand-picked hotels and restaurants, clearly organised by area, to suit all budgets and tastes. Select nightlife listings are also included here.

A–Z	98
ACCOMMODATION	108
RESTAURANTS	114
NIGHTLIFE	120

A-Z

A

ADDRESSES

Tokyo is divided into 23 *ku* (wards), which are subdivided into *cho* (districts), then numbered *chome* (blocks). Addresses in Japanese start with the city (outside of Tokyo it would be the *ken* or prefecture), followed by ward name, then district, city block and building numbers. For example, the address of the Tokyo Metropolitan Government Building would be written: Tokyo, Shinjuku-ku, Nishi-Shinjuku 2-8-1. This order is reversed when written in roman letters (the order used in this guide).

When navigating the city, Japanese people think in terms of city blocks, often finding their way from one to the next using landmarks. Even taxi drivers get confused away from the main thoroughfares.

B

BUDGETING

Tokyo need not be as expensive as you might fear. Staying at a hostel and eating cheaply can be done on a budget of ¥5,000 a day, although ¥10,000–15,000 is more reasonable. While five-star hotels can start from around ¥20,000 a night, there are plenty of mid-range options available for ¥8,000–15,000, sometimes with a light breakfast included. Lunchtime set-meal bargains can run to ¥1,000–2,000, and there are lots of inexpensive options such as noodle bars and revolving sushi restaurants. Drinking alcohol, though, can boost the bill substantially; the cheapest beer is typically around ¥700 a glass. Public transport is inexpensive, and entry to most attractions is reasonable.

The **GRUTT Pass** is a ¥2,000 ticket covering entry to 66 public, national and private institutions, including all Tokyo's major museums. It is valid for two months after first being used, and can be bought at participating venues and the Tokyo Tourist Information Centre in the Tokyo Metropolitan Government Building, Shinjuku *(see p.104)*.

C

CHILDREN

Although Tokyo is short on public parks and playgrounds, the city is like a giant hi-tech theme park in which kids are rollercoastered about on futuristic trains and monorails, greeted by flashing screens at every turn. Tokyo's safety, its abundant and clean public toilets, and its many pharmacies for infant necessities also make it a good choice for families.

For further English resources see www.tokyowithkids.com, an 'interactive online community for English-

Above: Senso-ji in Asakusa.

speaking parents in Tokyo'. Note that some of the information here can be out of date.

CLOTHING

Tokyoites are both highly fashionable and often quite formal in what they wear. Depending on the social occasion you might feel out of place if you dress too casually. Large *gaijin* (foreigners) will find it difficult to buy large-size clothes and shoes – for women this may even apply to anyone above petite. Slip-on shoes are best, as they will need to be removed on entering homes and some restaurants and other places. See also Etiquette, *p.100*. For climate information, *see p.12*.

CRIME AND SAFETY

Tokyo is one of the safest cities in the world, but visitors shouldn't become too nonchalant. Although rare, pickpocketing and muggings do happen, as do worse crimes. Police boxes *(koban)* can be found in all neighbourhoods, often near the major train stations.

CUSTOMS

Non-residents entering the country are given a duty-free allowance of 200 cigarettes, three 760ml bottles of alcohol, 2oz of perfume and gifts the total value of which is less than ¥200,000. For more information, see www.customs.go.jp.

D

DISABLED TRAVELLERS

While there is a drive to provide more accessible hotels, tourist facilities and public transport for disabled travellers, Tokyo is not an easy place for such people to get around. Useful, but outdated, information is available at http://accessible.jp.org.

E

EARTHQUAKES

Tokyo is notoriously susceptible to earthquakes. It is wise, therefore, to check the emergency exits in your hotel. In the event of a tremor, safety precautions include turning off any electrical or gas sources, opening exits, and standing or crouching under a sturdy door lintel or heavy table.

ELECTRICITY

The current in Tokyo is 100 volts AC, 50 cycles. American-style plugs with two flat pins are used. Adaptors and transformers are required if you come from countries like Britain where the voltage is 240.

EMBASSIES

Australia: 2-1-14 Mita, Minato-ku; tel: 5232 4111; www.australia.or.jp.

Carbon-Offsetting

Air travel produces a huge amount of carbon dioxide and is a significant contributor to global warming. If you would like to offset the damage caused to the environment by your flight, a number of organisations can do this for you using online 'carbon calculators' that tell you how much you need to donate. In the UK travellers can visit www.climatecare. org or www.carbon neutral.com; in the US log on to www. climatefriendly.com or www.sustainable travelinternational.org.

DIRECTORY

Internet

The internet can be accessed in most hotel rooms, either via LAN cable or wi-fi. Internet cafés can be found across the city, usually as part of 24-hour computer game and *manga* centres. For free wi-fi hotspots, see www.freespot.com/users/map_e.html.

Canada: 7-3-38 Akasaka, Minato-ku; tel: 5412 6200; www.canadanet.or.jp.
UK: 1 Ichiban-cho, Chiyoda-ku; tel: 5211 1100; http://ukinjapan.fco.gov.uk.
US: 1-10-5 Akasaka, Minato-ku; tel: 3224 5000; http://tokyo.usembassy.gov.

EMERGENCY NUMBERS

Ambulance and Fire: 119; Police: 110; Japan Helpline: 0120-461 997.

ETIQUETTE

While allowances are made for unschooled foreigners, a few pointers are useful, as some behaviour can cause genuine offence or embarrassment.
- Always remove your shoes before entering Japanese homes, inns and certain museums and restaurants. Rows of slippers at entrances indicate their use. Shoeboxes or lockers are other hints. Remove slippers before stepping onto *tatami* (woven straw) mats. You will also be required to switch slippers to a separate pair before entering a toilet.
- Blowing one's nose in public is a gross faux pas.
- When someone pours you a drink, you are expected to lift your glass slightly off the table and then pour the other person's drink.
- Chopsticks are never left sticking in rice, a gesture associated with the dead.

G

GAY & LESBIAN TRAVELLERS

Homosexuals tend to keep a low profile in Japan, and do not promote themselves in Tokyo as much as they do in other international cities. However, Tokyo is fairly tolerant of gay and alternative lifestyles, and has a thriving scene with a selection of clubs, events and support networks. It is mainly centred around Shinjuku in an area called Ni-chome, near to Shinjuku-Sanchome Station. Most of the bars, clubs and saunas here cater to the local gay community, but there are a number of places for non-Japanese-speakers *(see p.121)*.

Useful online starting points include GayNet Japan (http://gnj.jp) and Out Japan (www.outjapan.com/network).

GREEN ISSUES

With one of the world's best public transport networks, there are few places in Tokyo that are solely accessible by using a car or taxi. Separation and some recycling of trash is practised; you will find separate waste bins for burnable and non-burnable rubbish as well as cans, bottles and paper. Carry your own pair of chopsticks rather than using the disposable ones provided at almost every restaurant.

For information on carbon-offsetting your flights, *see margin, p.99*.

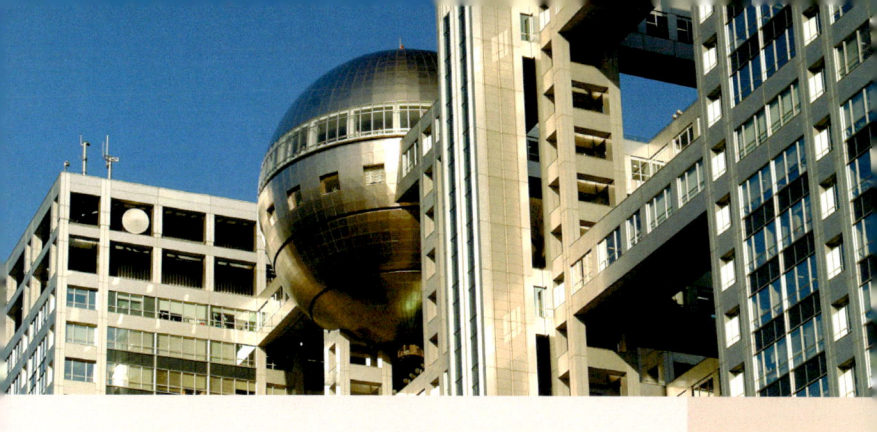

HEALTH & MEDICAL CARE

No vaccinations are required to enter Japan. Tap water is safe, and medical care is good. Hospitals and clinics with English-speaking staff include:
• Japanese Red Cross Medical Centre, 4-1-22 Hiro-o, Shibuya-ku; tel: 3400 1311; www.med.jrc.or.jp
• St Luke's International Hospital, 9-1 Akashicho, Chuo-ku; tel: 3541 5151; www.luke.or.jp
• Tokyo British Clinic, 2F Daikan-yama Y Building, 2-13-7 Ebisu-Nishi, Shibuya-ku; tel: 5458 6099; www.tokyobritishclinic.com
• Tokyo Medical and Surgical Clinic, 2F 32 Shiba-koen Building, 3-4-30 Shiba-koen, Minato-ku; tel: 3436 3028; www.tmsc.jp

HOURS AND HOLIDAYS

Officially, business hours are Mon–Fri 9am–5pm, but office workers often stay later. Shops open through the week, usually from around 10am to 7 or 8pm; many are open Sundays and closed another day of the week. Most restaurants open at around 11.30am and take last orders at about 9.30pm. Museums often close on Mondays. Restaurants, department stores and museums usually open on public holidays.

Public Holidays
1 Jan: New Year's Day
2nd Mon Jan: Coming of Age Day
11 Feb: Foundation Day
20–1 Mar: Spring Equinox
29 Apr: Green Day
3 May: Constitution Memorial Day
4 May: National Holiday
5 May: Children's Day
3rd Mon July: Marine Day
3rd Mon Sept: Respect the Aged Day
23–4 Sept: Autumn Equinox
2nd Mon Oct: Sports Day
3 Nov: Culture Day
23 Nov: Labour Day
23 Dec: Emperor's Birthday

LANGUAGE

With its three alphabets, Japanese is a notoriously difficult language to learn. However, don't let this put you off trying to master a few simple words and phrases. As a spoken language, Japanese is relatively easy to pronounce, and when used even in a basic form will often be greeted by the locals with joy. English is not widely spoken, but many people will understand written English, and it can be useful to write down what you're trying to communicate.

A list of simple words and phrases can be found on the pull-out map that accompanies this guide.

Above from far left: Tokyo City View in the Mori Tower at Roppongi Hills; Kenzo Tange's Fuji TV Building, Odaiba.

Lost Property
Chances are if you lose something in Tokyo, you will get it back. The train and subway systems both have highly efficient lost-property offices, as do many public buildings. Also check with the local police boxes *(koban)*, found in all neighbourhoods.

M

MAPS

Tourist offices provide adequate maps of the city for free. For more detail, buy the indispensable *Tokyo City Atlas: A Bilingual Guide*, published by Kondansha.

MEDIA

Newspapers and Magazines. Daily papers available in English include the *Japan Times* (www.japantimes.co.jp), the *International Herald Tribune* (www.asahi.com/english) and the *Daily Yomiuri* (www.yomiuri.co.jp/dy). Tokyo has several English-language listings magazines that can be picked up at the airport, in large English bookshops and hotels. The best is the free weekly *Metropolis* (http://metropolis.co.jp). Also worth a look are *Tokyo Weekender* (www.weekenderjapan.com) and the quarterly *Tokyo Journal* (www.tokyo.to).

Television and Radio. State broadcaster NHK offers NHK on channel 1, NHK Educational on channel 3 and the new NHK World channel (www.nhk.or.jp/nhkworld). The other main Tokyo channels are Nihon TV (channel 4), TBS (6), Fuji TV (8), TV Asahi (10) and TV Tokyo (12).

Samurai FM (www.samurai.fm) links up DJs in Tokyo and London. Radio Japan (www.nhk.or.jp/nhkworld) offers programmes in 18 different languages. Inter FM (76.1MHz; www.interfm.co.jp) has English-language news, and you can also hear English programming on J-WAVE (81.3MHz; www.j-wave music.com).

MONEY

The Japanese yen (¥) is available in 1-, 5-, 10-, 50-, 100- and 500-yen coins and 1,000, 2,000, 5,000 and 10,000 notes. Money can be exchanged at banks and authorised exchangers. Many shops do not accept credit cards, so carry a reasonable amount of cash. Major credit cards and cash cards linked to Cirrus, PLUS, Maestro and Visa Electron networks can be used at post office and Seven Bank (located at 7-Eleven stores) ATMs. Traveller's cheques are accepted by leading banks, hotels and stores.

P

POLICE

You can dial the police number (110) from any public phone, free of charge. Chances are, you won't have to walk more than a few blocks to find a local police box *(koban)*.

POST

Post offices are open Mon–Fri 9am–5pm; some are also open Sat 9am–3pm. For English-language information about postal services, including postal

POST

Above from far left: manga-style doll; public telephone sign; post box; Meiji-jingu.

fees, call 0570-046 111 or go to www.post.japanpost.jp. Tokyo Central Post Office (2-7-2 Marunouchi, Chiyoda-ku; tel: 3284 9539) is currently closed for reconstruction; try the nearby Tokyo International Post Office (2-3-3 Otemachi, Chiyoda-ku), which is open daily 24 hours.

R
RELIGION

Shinto is Japan's indigenous religion, an animist faith that involves the worship of spirits, or *kami*. Shinto shrines (indicated by the suffix *-jinja, -jingu* or *-gu*) are generally un-flamboyant in design, the most notable feature being the simple wooden *torii* gate, which symbolises a door between the earthly realm and that of the *kami*. In contrast, Buddhist temples (*-tera, -dera, -ji* or *-in*), such as Asakusa's Senso-ji, are more extravagant, with imposing entry gates flanked by fearsome statues of celestial guardians, or Nio.

T
TELEPHONES

Phone Numbers. Tokyo's area code is 03, but you don't need to dial this within the city. All regular telephone numbers have eight digits. Other area codes are Hakone: 0460, Kamakura: 0467, Kawagoe: 049, Narita: 0476 and Nikko: 0288.

Local numbers beginning with 0120, 0088 or 0053 are toll-free calls that can be dialled only within Japan.

If calling from one province to another, dial the area code first (with the zero).

International Calls. To dial Tokyo from the UK dial 00 (international code) + 81 (Japan) + area code (minus the initial 0) + the number. To call overseas from Tokyo, dial the access code of an international call-service provider (KDDI: 001, Japan Telecom: 0041, NTT: 0033, Cable & Wireless IDC: 0061), then the country code and the number.

For Directory Assistance.
• NTT Information Service – tel: 0120-505 506. In English.
• Local directory assistance – tel: 104. Ask for an English-speaking operator.
• International directory assistance (English-speaking) – tel: 0051.

Public Telephones. Public telephones take telephone cards, although some may accept ¥10 and ¥100 coins. Each carrier issues its own prepaid cards: NTT and DDI (domestic) and KDD (international). The cards can only be used at the appropriate telephone booth.

Mobile/Cell Phones. NTT DoCoMo (www.nttdocomo.com) and SoftBank Mobile (www.softbank-rental.jp) allow visitors to use their own numbers and SIM cards with their 3G services,

Smoking

This is banned in many public places, including on all public transport and in shops and public buildings. Restaurants and bars, however, do allow smoking, although many now do so in designated areas only. Smoking on the street is also being clamped down on in some of the inner-city wards, including Chuo-ku and Shinjuku-ku.

DIRECTORY **103**

although you will need to rent or buy a phone in Japan. Alternatively, rent a phone with a Japan-based number at Narita Airport to use during your stay. Most mobile numbers begin with 090.

TIME ZONES

Tokyo (like the rest of Japan) is +9 hours GMT, +14 hours EST (New York) and +17 PST (Los Angeles). Japan does not have summer daylight-saving time.

TIPPING

Tipping is not practised in Japan.

TOURIST INFORMATION

Japan National Tourist Organisation (JNTO; 2-10-1 Yurakucho, Chiyoda-ku; tel: 3216 1903; www.jnto.go.jp; Mon–Fri 9am–5pm, Sat 9am–noon) offers information on all of Japan as well as Tokyo. For city-specific details, visit the **Tokyo Tourist Information Centre** (1F Tokyo Metropolitan Government No. 1 Building, 2-8-1 Nishi-Shinjuku; tel: 5321 3077; daily 9.30am–6.30pm), also at **Haneda Airport** (tel: 5757 9345; daily 9am–10pm) and in the Kesei line station at **Ueno** (tel: 3836 3471; daily 9.30am–6.30pm).

The websites of the **Tokyo Convention and Visitors Bureau** (www.tcvb.or.jp) and the **Tokyo Metropolitan Government** (www.tourism.metro.tokyo.jp) have up-to-date information.

TRANSPORT

Arrival by Air

New Tokyo International Airport (Narita; tel: 0476-348 000; www.narita-airport.jp) is about 66km (40 miles) east of the city, and **Tokyo International Airport** (Haneda; tel: 5757 8111; www.tokyo-airport-bldg.co.jp) is 15km (10 miles) to the south. The city's two airports are usually referred to as Narita and Haneda. Most international flights arrive at Narita, but with the opening of a new runway, Haneda will see more flights to neighbouring countries.

Four big airlines serve Tokyo from the UK: British Airways, JAL, ANA and Virgin Atlantic. From the US or Canada, JAL and ANA, Northwest, American Airlines, Delta, Continental and United Airlines all have routes. Tokyo is also an increasingly important hub for flights to Asian destinations.

April, August and December tend to be the most expensive times to fly to Japan, as they coincide with the country's Golden Week, O-bon and Christmas-New Year holidays. Flying a few days either side of these peak periods can result in huge savings.

Narita Airport to City

Taxi. This is the most expensive option and usually the slowest. The fare to Tokyo is ¥20,000–30,000, but it's no quicker than the bus.

Limousine Bus. Frequent and comfortable airport limousine buses (tel:

Toilets
Public toilets can be found at most train and subway stations, as well as in department stores and shopping complexes. Occasionally you will come across squat toilets, but more often than not what you will find is a high-tech toilet, where the lid rises and falls as you enter and leave, and where there's no need for toilet paper (seldom provided in public toilets anyway – always be sure to carry a small supply yourself), since the contraption has wash and dry functions.

3665 7220; www.limousinebus.co.jp) are much cheaper than taxis; they cost ¥3,000 to most central Tokyo locations. The buses connect Narita Airport with most parts of the city, including major hotels, railway stations and Tokyo City Air Terminal (a pre-boarding check-in facility), as well as Haneda Airport and Tokyo Disneyland. Tickets can be bought in the arrivals lobby after clearing immigration and customs. Buses are boarded outside the terminal.

Train. This is the fastest way to reach Tokyo. Stations for the two competing express services are found on the basement level of both terminal buildings.

The **JR Narita Express** (tel: 3423 0111; www.jreast.co.jp/e/nex) connects with the JR railway network at Tokyo, Shinagawa, Shinjuku, Ikebukuro, Omiya, Yokohama and Ofuna stations. It takes an hour to Tokyo Station and the price is ¥2,940 for standard class.

The **Keisei Skyliner** (www.keisei.co.jp) runs to Tokyo's Ueno Station, stopping first at Nippori. The connection to JR lines or the subway at Ueno is not as convenient as the Narita Express, but the Skyliner is usually less crowded. It takes an hour to Ueno, costing ¥1,920.

Both the JR and Keisei lines offer cheaper but slower non-express train services to the city.

Haneda Airport to City

Taxi. It should take about 30 minutes to central Tokyo by taxi, costing around ¥5,000; but beware of traffic congestion.

Train. Most people opt for the cheaper trains. Frequent services run from the Keihin Kyuko Station in the airport basement. The train takes about 20 minutes to Shinagawa Station and costs ¥400.

Monorail. The Tokyo Monorail connects Haneda with Hamamatsucho Station on the JR Yamanote line. It takes only 17 minutes and costs ¥470, but can be very crowded.

Limousine Bus. An airport limousine bus service connects Haneda with central Tokyo. Fares start at ¥1,000, depending on which part of the city you are heading to. There is also a service from Haneda to Narita that takes about 75 minutes and costs ¥3,000.

Arrival by Road

Expressways are of extraordinarily high quality. Like in Britain, the Japanese drive on the left. Highway tolls are high, making trains and buses generally more economical.

Japan has an excellent system of **inter-city buses**. They are a comfortable and cheaper alternative to the bullet train. Buses include destinations not covered by trains, and many services are direct. Night buses are the cheapest, but leave late and arrive early. Some of these are operated by Japan Railways; buy tickets at the Green Window offices at JR stations.

The main JR bus office, where services from Kyoto and Osaka arrive, is on the Yaesu (east) side of Tokyo Station.

Above from far left: bullet trains; Hama Rikyu Garden.

Rail Passes
If you are planning to travel extensively around Japan, buying a JR Japan Rail Pass (www.japanrailpass.net) may be useful. You must buy it before you arrive in Japan, and it's valid for seven, 14 or 21 consecutive days. For travels closer to Tokyo, the JR East Pass (www.jreast.co.jp) is likely to be a better deal.

Arrival by Train

The majority of train lines entering Tokyo from major Japanese cities, whether regular or Shinkansen (bullet train), stop at Tokyo Station on the JR Yamanote line. Day trips to places like Hakone usually involve taking a private (non-JR) line. Most of these connect with major JR terminals like Shibuya and Shinjuku stations.

Transportation within Tokyo

Subway. Tokyo's clean, safe and convenient subway – made up of the nine-line **Tokyo Metro** (www.tokyometro.jp) and the four-line **Toei** (www.kotsu.metro.tokyo.jp) – is the fastest and most economical means of getting across town.

The two systems are fully integrated and run to precise schedules indicated on timetables posted at each station. Services run from 5am to 12.30am at intervals of 2–3 minutes during rush hours, with frequencies dropping to around every 5–10 minutes in off-peak periods. The frequency reduces slightly at weekends. All stations have a route map indicating fares for each stop near the ticket machines, usually in English.

Fares are regulated on a station-to-station basis, so if you cannot determine the fare required, just purchase the cheapest ticket available (¥160 for Tokyo Metro lines, ¥180 for Toei lines) at the ticket machine. Fare correction can be done on arrival.

Pasmo magnetic smart cards (www.pasmo.co.jp), good on any public transport line in Tokyo, can be bought at subway stations (¥500 deposit) and recharged when depleted. These are simply passed over sensors of the automated ticket gates as you enter, with the fare deducted at your destination. JR's Suica cards act in exactly the same way, and both can be used on subways, trains and buses.

Trains. Above ground, **Japan Railways** (JR) operate a service as efficient as the subway, with equivalent frequency and operating hours (5am–1am) on commuter lines. Like the subways, the lines are colour-coded.

The Yamanote line (green) makes a 35km (20-mile) oval loop around central Tokyo, with JR and private lines branching out to the suburbs. Also useful is the Chuo line (orange) that runs east–west, connecting Tokyo Station with Shinjuku Station and beyond. JR fares start at ¥130. Prepaid, chargeable Suica cards can be used instead of cash at ticket machines. A one-day Tokunai Pass (¥730) is good for unlimited JR train travel in central Tokyo.

Buses. There are no English signs on Tokyo buses, but imminent stops are announced by a recorded voice. Passengers pay on entry, dropping the flat fare (¥200) into a box located next to the driver; there's a machine in the box for changing notes if you don't have the coins. Tourist information centres and hotels can give you bus maps with

---

Discount Travel

Active sightseers can purchase a one-day economy pass (¥1,000) covering both metro systems, or a one-day Tokyo Combination Ticket (¥1,580) for use on all JR, metro and bus lines in the Tokyo region. Tickets are sold at pass offices at major stations.

the major routes marked. Buses generally run 5.30am–midnight.

Ferry. **Tokyo River Buses** (tel: 5733 4812; www.suijobus.co.jp) offer a range of services down the Sumida River and across Tokyo Bay. For details of their most popular route, connecting Asakusa and Hama Rikyu Garden, *see p.69*. Other routes include a cruise around Tokyo Harbour (45 min), past Rainbow Bridge to Kasai Sealife Park (55 min), and to the Shinagawa Aquarium (35 min). All boats depart from Hinode Pier, near Takeshiba Station on the Yurikamome line. Look out for the striking, sci-fi-esque *Himiko* vessel, designed by *manga* artist Leiji Matsumoto, which morphs into the floating bar Jicoo at night (www.jicoofloatingbar.com).

Taxis. Taxis are a convenient but pricey way of getting around. The standard flagfall in Tokyo is ¥700; anything other than short trips can run from ¥3,000 to ¥5,000. No tipping is expected.

Taxis are readily available on the streets, and at every major hotel and railway station. A red light in the front window signifies that the taxi is available. Roads are narrow and traffic congestion is appalling at rush hour.

Most taxi drivers speak only Japanese, so it helps to have your destination written down in Japanese. Do not be surprised if taxis fail to stop when you hail them, particularly at night. Drivers will be looking for profitable runs to the suburbs rather than foreigners wanting to return to their hotels.

Note that there is no need to touch the door when getting in or out of taxi – they are automatically opened and closed by the driver.

Recommended taxi operators are:
Hinomaru: tel: 3212 0505; www.hinomaru.co.jp/taxi
Nihon Kotsu: tel: 5755 2336; www.nihon-kotsu.co.jp

Driving and Car Rental. Tokyo is not an easy place in which to drive. Except on the often crowded expressways, there are few road signs in romanised Japanese, and parking is always a problem. For getting out of town, it is usually faster to take public transport. If you do need to hire a car, try **Toyota Rent-a-Car** (http://rent.toyota.co.jp), which has branches at the airports and across the city.

V

VISAS

Nationals of most Western countries do not need a visa for a short visit. On arrival, visitors are usually granted temporary visitor status, good for 90 days. Anyone wishing to extend their stay should visit the Tokyo Regional Immigration Bureau office (5-5-30 Konan, Minato-ku; tel: 5796 7112; www.moj.go.jp).

Above from far left: Tokyo has a very efficient subway system; taxis in Ginza.

Bicycle Rental
Intrepid travellers may want to try cycling around Tokyo. Major roads can be perilous, but if you stick to the back roads, bikes offer a great way to get intimate with the city at surface level. Try Cool Bike (tel: 3260 6316; www.coolbike.jp), which charges ¥2,000 a day; for an extra ¥2,000 they will deliver their folding bikes to your hotel. A good website for further information is Cycle Tokyo (http://cycle-tokyo.cycling.jp). *See also feature, p.13.*

ACCOMMODATION

There is no lack of places to stay in Tokyo, with some of the world's top brands in the market. Accommodation ranges from de-luxe palaces to no-frills business lodgings and budget 'capsule hotels'. Older establishments exude a distinctive Japanese ambience, while business hotels come with clean and functional bedrooms.

The best traditional Japanese inns, or *ryokan*, epitomise the essence of Japanese hospitality. You sleep on futon mattresses on *tatami* mats, bathe in a traditional bath and are served exquisite *kaiseki ryori* meals in your room by attendants in kimonos. Note that they often don't accept credit cards; if staying at one, it is best to check in advance.

Capsule hotels have become a famous symbol of crowded Japan. Located near big stations, they provide fully equipped sleeping cells at economic rates, mostly for drunken men who miss the last train home to the suburbs.

Marunouchi & Ginza

Imperial Hotel
1-1-1 Uchisaiwai-cho, Chiyoda-ku; tel: 3504 1111; www.imperialhotel.co.jp; station: Hibiya; ¥¥¥¥
Japan's first Western-style hotel (1890), now in its third incarnation, offers top service and restful rooms. Its central location near Hibiya Park, the Imperial Palace and the chic Ginza shopping area makes it a favourite of travellers and businesspeople alike.

The Peninsula Tokyo
1-8-1 Yurakucho, Chiyoda-ku; tel: 6270 2888; www.peninsula.com; stations: Hibiya or Yurakucho; ¥¥¥¥
A branch of the Hong Kong flagship, the Peninsula's superb location and high-class style are hard to match. Try to get one of the middle- or upper-level rooms, which have outstanding views.

Yaesu Fujiya Hotel
2-9-1 Yaesu, Chuo-ku; tel: 3273 2111; www.yaesufujiya.com; station: Tokyo; ¥¥
This two-decade-old hotel has some elegant touches, like its majestic red-carpeted staircase descending into the lobby. Rooms are relatively small, but each has cable TV with CNN access.

Yaesu Terminal Hotel
1-5-14 Yaesu, Chuo-ku; tel: 3281 3771; www.yth.jp; station: Tokyo; ¥¥
The rooms in this business hotel may be on the small side, but they are clean and good value for the area.

Roppongi & Akasaka

Akasaka Excel Hotel Tokyu
2-14-3 Nagatacho, Chiyoda-ku; tel: 3580 2311; www.tokyuhotelsjapan.com; station: Akasaka-Mitsuke; ¥¥¥
Offers reliable quality, efficient service and reasonable rates compared to the nearby luxury hotels. Rooms away from the road are quieter. There are good shops and restaurants in the downstairs mall, and bars on the upper levels.

Arca Torre

6-1-23 Roppongi, Minato-ku; tel: 3404 5111; www.arktower.co.jp/arcatorre; station: Roppongi; ¥¥

Close to the busy Roppongi Crossing, this place can be a little noisy at times and is certainly at the heart of the action. Standard single rooms boast large semi-double beds, and there are helpful multilingual staff.

Asia Center of Japan Hotel

8-10-32 Akasaka, Minato-ku; tel: 3402 6111; www.asiacenter.or.jp; station: Nogizaka; ¥

Book well ahead for this popular lodging for low-budget travellers. Rooms in the newer wing are a notch up from the older cramped ones. A few minutes' walk from the subway, the location is good for both the Roppongi and Aoyoma areas.

Chisun Grand Akasaka

6-3-17 Akasaka, Minato-ku; tel: 5572 7788; www.solarehotels.com; station: Akasaka; ¥¥

This flagship of the good-value Chisun chain of business hotels offers appealing rooms decorated in browns and reds, and extra-spacious bathrooms for a business hotel.

Grand Hyatt

6-10-3 Roppongi, Minato-ku; tel: 4333 1234; http://tokyo.grand.hyatt.com; station: Roppongi; ¥¥¥¥

Truly spectacular, but in an understated manner. Wood, glass and marble in the public areas form clutter-free and contemporary lines. Bedrooms feature flat-screen televisions (including one in the bathroom), CD players and high-speed internet, plus capacious bathrooms.

New Otani

4-1 Kioi-cho, Chiyoda-ku; tel: 3265 1111; www.newotani.co.jp; station: Akasaka; ¥¥¥¥

A massive complex with many restaurants and extensive Japanese gardens that are worth seeing in their own right. On the borderline with Akasaka, but within a 10-minute walk of the Imperial Palace, the location is ideal for both sightseeing and nightlife.

Okura

2-10-4 Toranomon, Minato-ku; tel: 3582 0111; www.okura.com; station: Roppongi-Itchome; ¥¥¥¥

Long held to be one of the world's great hotels, the Okura offers an atmospheric blend of traditional Japanese decor and 21st-century facilities, including an excellent range of restaurants.

Above from far left: New Otani; The Peninsula Tokyo.

Hotel Charges

Western-style hotels charge on a per-room basis, although at traditional *ryokan* inns and pensions customers are charged per person with the rate usually including dinner and breakfast. Many larger hotels also offer non-smoking rooms and women-only floors. All hotel rates include 5 percent consumption tax. Luxury hotels may impose a 10–15 percent service charge. If your room costs over ¥10,000 per person per night, there's also a Tokyo Metropolitan Government tax of ¥100 per person per night (¥200 per person if the room costs over ¥15,000).

Price for a double room for one night without breakfast:

¥¥¥¥	over ¥30,000
¥¥¥	¥20,000–30,000
¥¥	¥10,000–20,000
¥	below ¥10,000

Ritz Carlton

Tokyo Midtown, 9-7-1 Akasaka, Minato-ku; tel: 3423 8000; www.ritzcarlton.com; station: Roppongi; ¥¥¥¥

Occupying the top nine floors of the Midtown Tower is this ultra-luxury hotel. Beautifully decorated and spacious rooms are complemented by the Ritz's famous afternoon teatime service, with bird's-eye views of Tokyo from the Lobby Lounge and Bar on the 45th floor.

Hotel Villa Fontaine Roppongi

1-6-2 Roppongi, Minato-ku; tel: 3560 1110; www.villa-fontaine.co.jp; station: Roppongi-itchome; ¥¥

One in the chain of excellent-value, stylish business hotels. Offers rooms larger than most in this category, a complimentary buffet breakfast and discounted rates at weekends.

Aoyama

Hotel Floracion

4-17-58 Minami-Aoyama, Minato-ku; tel: 3403 1541; www.floracion-aoyama.com; station: Omotesando; ¥¥¥

Aoyama is short on hotels, but this one, tucked away in the backstreets off Omotesando, is worth searching out. It offers good-quality Western-style rooms and pleasant service.

Shibuya

Arimax

11-15, Kamiyama-cho, Shibuya-ku; tel: 5454 1122; station: Shibuya; ¥¥¥

A small hotel with an elite European feel and intimate atmosphere, it offers neoclassical and English Regency-style rooms with full facilities. A quick 10-minute walk west of JR Shibuya Station's Hachiko exit.

Cerulean Tower Tokyu Hotel

26-1 Sakuragaoka-cho, Shibuya-ku; tel: 3476 3000; www.ceruleantower-hotel.com; station: Shibuya; ¥¥¥¥

Shibuya's most upmarket hotel covers the 19th to 37th floors of a tower, offering splendid views. The rooms are spacious, fully equipped and tastefully decorated. On the premises are bars and several Japanese and Western eating options, including a modern *kaiseki ryori* restaurant and *noh* theatre.

Shibuya City Hotel

1-1 Maruyamacho, Shibuya-ku; tel: 5489 1010; www.shibuya-city-hotel.com; station: Shibuya; ¥¥

This small business hotel, under 10 minutes from Shibuya Station and opposite the Bunkamura complex, is

---

Useful Websites
- Japan Hotel Association (www.j-hotel.or.jp)
- Japan Hotel Net (www.japanhotel.net)
- Japan Ryokan Association (www.ryokan.or.jp)
- Japan Ryokan & Hotel Association (www.nikkanren.or.jp)
- Japan Guest Houses (www.japaneseguesthouses.com)

Price for a double room for one night without breakfast:

¥¥¥¥	over ¥30,000
¥¥¥	¥20,000–30,000
¥¥	¥10,000–20,000
¥	below ¥10,000

ideally located for taking in the arts, shopping and nightlife of Shibuya.

Shibuya Excel Tokyu

1-12-2 Dogenzaka, Shibuya-ku; tel: 5457 0109; www.tokyuhotels japan.com; station: Shibuya; ¥¥

This well-priced hotel for business travellers is part of the Mark City complex attached to Shibuya Station. It offers two floors solely for women, as well as a bar, restaurants and all the amenities you would expect from this hotel chain.

Shinjuku

Green Plaza Capsule Hotel

1-29-2 Kabuki-cho, Shinjuku-ku; tel: 5457 0109; www.hgpshinjuku.jp; station: Shinjuku; ¥

Claiming to be Tokyo's very first capsule hotel, this men-only operation is one of the best of its kind. Located in the heart of Kabuki-cho, it's surprisingly comfortable once you get used to the idea of being supine in a plastic case. Features an outdoor bath and restaurant.

Hyatt Regency Tokyo

2-7-2 Nishi-Shinjuku, Shinjuku-ku; tel: 3348 1234; www.tokyo.regency. hyatt.com; stations: Shinjuku or Tochomae; ¥¥¥¥

In the heart of West Shinjuku, this is one of Tokyo's most praised hotels, although you wouldn't realise it from the outside. The interior, with its soaring atrium lobby, is a different story. The posh executive floors are exclusive, with separate facilities and king-sized beds.

Kadoya Hotel

1-23-1 Nishi-Shinjuku, Shinjuku-ku; tel: 3346 2561; www.kadoya-hotel.co.jp; stations: Shinjuku or Tochomae; ¥¥

A super business hotel that's a bargain for the location. There's internet access, a good *izakaya* (restaurant-pub) in the basement and English-speaking staff.

Keio Plaza Hotel

2-2-1 Nishi-Shinjuku, Shinjuku-ku; tel: 3344 0111; www.keioplaza. co.jp; stations: Shinjuku or Tochomae; ¥¥¥

This large 45-storey skyscraper in West Shinjuku is long established and well maintained, with a health club, outdoor swimming pool, business facilities and an array of fine restaurants and bars.

Park Hyatt Tokyo

3-7-1-2 Nishi-Shinjuku, Shinjuku-ku; tel: 5322 1234; www.tokyo.park. hyatt.com; station: Tochomae; ¥¥¥¥

Made famous when the movie *Lost in Translation* was shot here, this de-luxe property has a fantastic setting on the top 14 floors of the 52-storey Park Tower. Expect top-class facilities and superb service. Home to the excellent New York Grill restaurant. *See also p.51.*

Above from far left: view from the Park Hyatt's New York Grill; even the hotel's bathrooms have great views.

Tokyo International Youth Hostel

Central Plaza, 18F, 21-1 Kagurakashi, Shinjuku-ku; tel: 3235 1107; www.tokyo-ih.jp; station: Iidabashi; ¥

If you don't mind sharing a room, the clean dormitory-style bunk beds at this eco-friendly youth hostel right next to JR Iidabashi Station may suit. There's no access to the building between 10am and 3pm, and also an 11pm curfew.

Yanaka & Ueno

Ryokan Katsutaro Annex

3-8-4 Yanaka, Taito-ku; tel: 3828 2500; www.katsutaro.com/annex_rate.html; station: Sendagi; ¥¥

This modern *ryokan* combines the best of Japanese decor, with *tatami* flooring and paper-screen windows. There are also private bathrooms and broadband internet access in each room, along with free internet usage and coffee in the entrance area. The hotel is located just around the corner from Yanaka Ginza, a lively street with crafts and teashops.

Sawanoya Ryokan

2-3-11 Yanaka, Taito-ku; tel: 3822 2251; www.tctv.ne.jp/members/sawanoya; station: Nezu; ¥

This friendly, family-run *ryokan*, situated in a residential neighbourhood close to the old quarter of Yanaka, offers small but comfortable rooms with *tatami* mats. The ¥300 self-service breakfast is good value. It's about a seven-minute walk from Nezu Station.

Ueno First City Hotel

1-14-8 Ueno, Taito-ku; tel: 3831 8215; www.uenocity-hotel.com; station: Yushima; ¥¥

This smart business hotel with a red-brick façade prides itself on its comfort and efficiency. It's located within walking distance of both Ueno and the area around the Yushima Tenjin shrine. The restaurant, bar and coffee shop are as intimate as the hotel itself.

Ikebukuro & Mejirodai

Chinzan-so Four Seasons Hotel

Chinzan-so, 2-10-8 Sekiguchi, Bunkyo-ku; tel: 3943 2222; www.fourseasons.com/tokyo; station: Edogawabashi; ¥¥¥¥

A superlative low-rise hotel overlooking the woodlands of the Chinzan-so garden, with its pagoda, waterfall and Buddhist statuary. Western luxury is combined with Japanese attention to detail. A drawback is the rather remote location, a 10-minute walk from Edogawabashi Station.

Kimi Ryokan

2-36-8 Ikebukuro, Toshima-ku; tel: 3971 3766; www.kimi-ryokan.jp; station: Ikebukuro; ¥

This homely *ryokan* is one of Tokyo's best-loved budget stays, with helpful English-speaking staff. It's very popular, so book in advance. Located in a quiet backstreet off Tokiwa-dori, the *ryokan* is a 10-minute walk to the JR station.

Hotel Metropolitan

1-6-1 Nishi-Ikebukuro, Toshima-ku; tel: 3980 1111; www.metropolitan.jp; station: Ikebukuro; ¥¥¥

A plush hotel with comfortable, good-sized rooms, several restaurants and an outdoor pool (mid-June–early Sept).

Asakusa

Asakusa View Hotel

3-17-1 Nishi-Asakusa, Taito-ku; tel: 3847 1111; www.viewhotels.co.jp/asakusa; station: Asakusa; ¥¥

Well situated for sightseeing and shopping in downtown Asakusa, this hotel has Western-style rooms that offer good views – as does the bar on the 28th floor.

Ryokan Shigetsu

1-31-11 Asakusa, Taito-ku; tel: 3843 2345; www.shigetsu.com; station: Asakusa; ¥¥

Steps away from Nakamise-dori, this is one of Asakusa's nicest *ryokan* offerings, with small Western- or Japanese-style rooms, all en suite. The top-floor bath offers views over the nearby temple roofs.

Sukeroku-no-yado Sadachiyo

2-20-1 Asakusa, Taito-ku; tel: 3842 6431; www.sadachiyo.co.jp; stations: Asakusa or Tawaramachi; ¥¥

Close by Senso-ji, this is an atmospheric *ryokan* where the traditions of old Edo are maintained. All the *tatami* rooms have en-suite bathrooms, but there are also traditional-style larger communal baths.

Tsukiji & Odaiba

Conrad Hotel

1-9-1 Higashi-Shimbashi, Minato-ku; tel: 6388 8000; www.conradtokyo.co.jp; station: Shimbashi; ¥¥¥¥

Shiodome's high-end accommodation doesn't come more luxurious than this. Immaculate service from multilingual staff, designer rooms with hardwood finishing and views across the Hama-Rikyu Garden and Tokyo Bay. It's also within walking distance of Tsukiji Fish Market.

Nikko Tokyo

1-9-1 Daiba, Minato-ku; tel: 5500 5511; www.hnt.co.jp; station: Odaiba; ¥¥¥¥

In front of Odaiba Station on the Yurikamome line, the Nikko has one of the best views of the waterfront. The terrace restaurant and Captain's Bar are romantic settings popular with couples. Provides first-rate service and food, plus convenient access to all Odaiba sights.

Above from far left: Nikko Tokyo inside and out.

Price for a double room for one night without breakfast:	
¥¥¥¥	over ¥30,000
¥¥¥	¥20,000–30,000
¥¥	¥10,000–20,000
¥	below ¥10,000

RESTAURANTS

Most restaurants close between lunch and dinner. English-language menus are not common, but many eateries have plastic food displays in their windows. For up-to-date information on Tokyo's dynamic restaurant scene, check out the Tokyo Food Page (www.bento.com) or the reviews in *Metropolis* (http://metropolis.co.jp).

Marunouchi & Ginza

Bird Land

B1F Tsukamoto Sozan Building, 4-2-15 Ginza, Chuo-ku; tel: 5250 1081; Tue–Sat 5–9.30pm; station: Ginza; ¥¥¥

Top-quality *yakitori* (grilled skewers of chicken), made with free-range chicken grilled over charcoal. Don't miss the *sansai-yaki* (chicken breast grilled with Japanese pepper). Reservations advised.

Dhaba India

2-7-9 Yaesu, Chuo-ku; tel: 3272 7160; www.dhabaindia.com; Mon–Fri 11.15am–3pm and 5–11pm, Sat–Sun noon–3pm and 5–10pm; station: Kyobashi; ¥¥

Fragrant curries, generous thali meals and masala dhosas. The best South Indian cuisine in the city.

Little Okinawa

8-7-10 Ginza, Chuo-ku; tel: 3572 2930; Mon–Fri 5pm–3am, Sat–Sun 4pm–midnight; station: Shinbashi; ¥¥¥

This cosy bar-restaurant showcases the food of subtropical Okinawa. Plenty of pork, stir-fries featuring bitter melon, and Chinese-style noodles, all washed down with potent *awamori* liquor.

Locanda Elio

2-5-2 Kojimachi, Chiyoda-ku; tel: 3239 6771; www.elio.co.jp; Mon–Sat 11.45am–3pm and 5.45–11pm; station: Hanzomon; ¥¥¥

Elio Orsara's fresh pasta, Calabrian country soups and excellent southern Italian food come highly recommended.

Rangetsu

3-5-8 Ginza, Chuo-ku; tel: 3567 1021; www.ginza-rangetsu.com; daily 11.30am–10pm; station: Ginza; ¥¥¥¥

Refined Japanese cuisine based around *shabu-shabu* (hotpot) and *sukiyaki* (one-pot meal), featuring premium Wagyu beef cooked at the table.

Sakyo Higashiyama

B1F Oak Ginza, 3-7-2 Ginza, Chuo-ku; tel: 3535 3577; daily 11am–2pm and 5.30–9pm; station: Ginza; ¥¥¥

Sophisticated Kyoto cuisine without airs or graces. Fish and meat dishes prepared over charcoal in a sand pot.

Salt

5F Shin-Marunouchi Building, 1-5-1 Marunouchi, Chiyoda-ku; tel: 5288 7828; www.pj-world.com/salt; daily 11am–3.30pm and 5.30–11pm; station: Tokyo; ¥¥¥

Australian celebrity-chef Luke Mangan's venture features fabulous seafood and a fine cellar of Antipodean wines in a sleek setting. Attached is the **W.W wine bar** (tel: 5288-7829). In the same building on the seventh floor is **Marunouchi-House** (www.marunouchi-house.com), a series of casual restaurants, cafés and bars with access to a broad terrace.

Ten-Ichi Deux

4-1 Ginza, Chuo-ku; tel: 3566 4188; daily 11.30am–10pm; station: Ginza; ¥¥

An affordable offshoot of Tokyo's best-known tempura house, serving simple meals of deep-fried battered seafood and vegetables in a stylish ambience.

Roppongi & Akasaka

L'Atelier de Joël Robuchon

2F, Roppongi Hills Hillside, 6-10-1 Roppongi, Minato-ku; tel: 5772 7500; daily 11.30am–2.30pm and 6–11pm; station: Roppongi; ¥¥¥

Robuchon's tapas-influenced cuisine blends informal and sophisticated, but need not break the bank. Counter seating looking into the open kitchen.

Butagumi

2-24-9 Nishi-Azabu, Minato-ku; tel: 5466 6775; Tue–Sun 11.30am–3pm and 5.30–11pm; station: Roppongi; ¥¥

A traditional setting for one of Tokyo's finest renditions of *tonkatsu* – deep-fried, breaded premium pork cutlets. Choose fatty *rosu* or lean filet or Iberian. English spoken.

Chinese Café Eight

2F, Court Annex, 3-2-13 Nishi-Azabu, Minato-ku; tel: 5414 5708; www.chinesecafe8.com; daily 24 hours; station: Roppongi; ¥¥

Budget Chinese diner open round the clock, serving Peking duck (for three or four people) dumplings and simple stir-fries at bargain prices. They also have branches in Ebisu and Akasaka.

Fukuzushi

5-7-8 Roppongi, Minato-ku; tel: 3402 4116; www.roppongifukuzushi.com; Mon–Sat 11.30am–2pm and 5.30–11pm; station: Roppongi; ¥¥¥¥

Unfailingly good-quality sushi for the well-heeled Roppongi crowd. Expensive, but not snobbish or exclusive.

Inakaya East

5-3-4 Roppongi, Minato-ku; tel: 3408 5040; www.roppongiinakaya.jp; daily 5–11pm; station: Roppongi; ¥¥¥¥

Chefs in traditional garb grill fish, meat and vegetables to order, then pass them on long wooden paddles across to where you are sitting. It's theatrical and fun, but not cheap.

Above from far left: chilled udon noodles with shredded seaweed and grated *daikon* radish; sushi chefs at Fukuzushi; seafood soup.

Prices for a three-course meal, excluding beverages:	
¥¥¥¥	over ¥5,000
¥¥¥	¥3,000–5,000
¥¥	¥1,000–3,000
¥	below ¥1,000

Ninja

1F, Akasaka Tokyu Plaza, 2-14-3 Nagatacho, Chiyoda-ku; tel: 5157 3936; www.ninjaakasaka.com; Mon–Sat 5pm–2am, Sun 5–11pm; station: Akasaka; ¥¥¥

In this theme-restaurant black-clad waiters dressed like ninja spies show you to your private room, then entertain you as you nibble on simple Japanese food. Lots of fun for all the family.

Nodaiwa

1-5-4 Higashi-Azabu, Minato-ku; tel: 3583 7852; Mon–Sat 11am–1.30pm and 5–8pm; station: Kamiyacho; ¥¥¥

Charcoal-grilled fillets of *unagi* (eel) are daubed with a savoury sauce and served with rice. This is one of best places in Tokyo to try this unsung delicacy of Japanese cuisine.

Roy's

5F West Walk Roppongi Hills, 6-10-1 Roppongi, Minato-ku; tel: 5413 9571; daily 11.30am–4pm and 5.30–11.30pm; station: Roppongi; ¥¥¥¥

Roy Yamaguchi (one of Hawaii's top chefs) brings his delectable Asian-American cuisine to Tokyo. There's a stunning setting, too, with a panorama of Tokyo Tower.

Tofuya Ukai

4-4-13 Shiba Koen, Minato-ku; tel: 3436 1028; www.ukai.co.jp; daily 11am–8pm; station: Akebanebashi; ¥¥¥¥

Right below Tokyo Tower, this remarkable restaurant boasts traditional architecture and a beautiful rambling garden with carp ponds. Refined multi-course meals based around tofu are served in private rooms; fully vegetarian food is available by request.

Aoyama & Harajuku

L'Artemis

2-31-7 Jingumae, Shibuya-ku; tel: 5786 0220; Thur–Tue noon–3pm, 6–11pm, closed 2nd Tue of month; stations: Harajuku or Meiji-jingumae; ¥¥¥

Excellent, affordable French cuisine worthy of far grander surroundings. Chef Nakada's three-course dinner menu is a steal.

Jap Cho Ok

B1F Alteka Belte Plaza, 4-1-15 Minami-Aoyama, Minato-ku; tel: 5410 3408; www.1999group.com/zassouya; Mon–Sat 5.30pm–2am, Sun and hols 5.30–11pm; station: Gaienmae; ¥¥

Stylish yet casual, Jap Cho Ok features seafood dishes and even Zen Buddhist vegetarian temple cooking alongside the usual Korean barbecue. Great decor.

Sasagin

1-32-15 Yoyogi-Uehara, Shibuya-ku; tel: 5454 3715; Mon–Sat 5–11pm; station: Yoyogi-uehara; ¥¥¥

A range of premium sake is served with creative modern Japanese cuisine in a casual setting. The master speaks English and will recommend the best brews.

Above from far left: stylish Jap Cho Ok; open kitchens reveal craftsmen at work.

Shibuya & Ebisu

Beacon
1-2-5 Shibuya, Shibuya-ku; tel: 6418 0077; www.tyharborbrewing.co.jp/restaurants/beacon.html; Mon–Fri 11.30am–3pm and 6–10pm, Sat–Sun until 9pm; stations: Shibuya or Omotesando; ¥¥¥¥

One of the best steakhouses in the city, a sleek 'urban chop house' with good seafood and free-range chicken, and a huge cellar of Californian wines. Perfect for expense-account entertaining.

Buri
1-14-1 Ebisu-Nishi, Shibuya-ku; tel: 3496 7744; www.to-vi.jp; daily 5pm–3am; station: Ebisu; ¥¥

Great sake and tasty food at this standing-only bar that's good for late-night snacking.

Soranoniwa
4-17 Sakuragaoka-cho, Shibuya-ku; tel: 5728 5191; daily 5–11.30pm; station: Shibuya; ¥¥¥

Simple and affordable tofu cuisine. Highlights are tofu *shumai* dumplings and *yuba* (soya milk 'skin') prepared at the table. English menu.

Prices for a three-course meal, excluding beverages:

¥¥¥¥	over ¥5,000
¥¥¥	¥3,000–5,000
¥¥	¥1,000–3,000
¥	below ¥1,000

Sushi Ouchi
2-8-4 Shibuya, Shibuya-ku; tel: 3407 3543; Mon–Sat 11.30am–1.30pm, 5.30–9.30pm; stations: Shibuya and Omotesando; ¥¥¥

Chef Ouchi plays classical music and prefers a dark-wood decor. All-natural ingredients: no farmed seafood and absolutely no MSG or other chemicals.

Shinjuku

Carmine Edochiano
9-13 Arakicho, Shinjuku-ku; tel: 3225 6767; www.carmine.jp; daily 11.30am–3pm and 6–11pm; station: Yotsuya-Sanchome; ¥¥¥

Classy Italian fare in a beautiful old house. Dine upstairs on Tuscan cuisine; downstairs serves Neapolitan pizzas from a wood-fired oven.

Le Coupe Chou
1-15-7 Nishi-Shinjuku, Shinjuku-ku; tel: 3348 1610; daily 11.30am–2pm and 5.30pm–midnight, closed 3rd Mon of month; station: Shinjuku; ¥¥

In West Shinjuku's electronics district, this cosy, retro French bistro offers a great-value four-course lunch. Popular with the local office crowd.

Hayashi
2-22-5 Kabuki-cho, Shinjuku-ku; tel: 3209 5672; Mon–Sat 5–11.30pm; station: Shinjuku; ¥¥

Around the sand hearth, dine on charcoal-grilled meat, fish or seasonal vegetables in a rustic setting.

DIRECTORY 117

Hyakunincho Yataimura

2-20-25 Hyakunin-cho, Shinjuku-ku; tel: 5386 3320; Sun–Thur 11.30am–2.30pm and 5pm–2am, Fri–Sat until 4am; station: Shin-Okubo; ¥

Southeast Asian-style low-budget street-food court; choose from Indonesian, Thai, Korean and others. Tucked away on the back streets, it's open until the wee hours.

Matsuya

1-1-17 Okubo, Shinjuku-ku; tel: 3200 5733; Mon–Sat 11am–5am, Sun 11am–2am; station: Shin-Okubo; ¥

A long-established restaurant in Tokyo's Little Seoul, where you sit on the floor at low tables. The speciality is fiery meat-laden stews cooked at the table.

Yanaka & Ueno

Bon

1-2-11 Ryusen, Taito-ku; tel: 3872 0375; www.fuchabon.co.jp; Mon–Fri noon–3pm, 5–9pm, Sat noon–9pm, Sun noon–8pm; station: Iriya; ¥¥¥¥

Memorable multi-course *fucha ryori* (Buddhist vegetarian cuisine), featuring exquisitely prepared seasonal foods in a serene setting. Set menu changes with the seasons.

Ikenohata Yabu Soba

3-44-7 Yushima, Bunkyo-ku; tel: 3831 8977; Mon–Tue, Thur–Sat 11.30am–2pm and 4.30–8pm, Sun 11.30am–8pm; station: Yushima; ¥¥

Serves simple, filling and affordable light meals of *soba* noodles. English menu available.

Nezu Club

2-30-2 Nezu, Bunkyo-ku; tel: 3828 4004; www.nezuclub.com; Thur–Sun 6–10pm; station: Nezu; ¥¥¥¥

A delightful place in one of Tokyo's most traditional neighbourhoods, Nezu Club dishes up contemporary Japanese cuisine midway between formal and home cooking.

Sasanoyuki

2-15-10 Negishi, Taito-ku; tel: 3873 1145; www.sasanoyuki.com; Tue–Sun 11.30am–10pm; station: Uguisudani; ¥¥¥

Tokyo's most historic tofu restaurant is simple and relaxed, with reasonable prices. The set courses here can be quite filling.

Ikebukuro & Mejirodai

Chion Shokudo

B1F Miyakawa Building, 1-24-1 Ikebukuro, Toshima-ku; tel: 5951 8288; daily 11am–3am; station: Ikebukuro; ¥¥

Prices for a three-course meal, excluding beverages:	
¥¥¥¥	over ¥5,000
¥¥¥	¥3,000–5,000
¥¥	¥1,000–3,000
¥	below ¥1,000

Also known as Zhiyin Shitang, this restaurant specialises in fiery Sichuan fare such as *mabo-dofu* (ground pork and tofu) and spicy hotpots, as authentic (and almost as cheap) as you would find in China.

Goemon
1-1-26 Hon-Komagome, Toshima-ku; tel: 3811 2015; Tue–Fri noon–2pm and 5–10pm, Sat–Sun noon–8pm; stations: Hakusan or Hon-Komagome; ¥¥¥

Serving multi-course menus based around tofu, in a traditional setting overlooking a tranquil garden, this is one of Tokyo's most charming restaurants.

Saigon
3F, Torikoma Dai-ichi Building, 1-7-10 Higashi-Ikebukuro, Toshima-ku; tel: 3989 0255; Mon–Fri 11.30am–2.30pm and 5–10.30pm, Sat–Sun and hols 11.30am–10.30pm; station: Ikebukuro; ¥¥

Serves down-to-earth Vietnamese fare, including spring rolls, hot pancakes with spicy sauce and beef noodle soup. Set lunches for under ¥1,000.

Sasashu
2-2-6 Ikebukuro, Toshima-ku; tel: 3971 6796; Mon–Sat 5–11pm; station: Ikebukuro; ¥¥¥

This long-established *izakaya* (restaurant-tavern) serves premium sake, with a range of traditional food. Try the excellent duck noodles.

Asakusa

Ichimon
3-12-6 Asakusa, Taito-ku; tel: 3875 6800; Mon–Fri 6–11pm, Sat–Sun noon–2pm and 5–10pm; station: Asakusa; ¥¥¥

An atmospheric, well-placed old-world restaurant. Offers excellent sake and a good selection of Japanese dishes.

Otafuku
1-6-2 Senzoku, Taito-ku; tel: 3871 2521; Tue–Sun 5–11pm; station: Iriya; ¥¥

This venerable restaurant serves *oden* – chunky pieces of fishcake and vegetables simmered in stock – and pine-scented sake.

Tsukiji & Odaiba

Edogin
4-5-1 Tsukiji, Chuo-ku; tel: 3543 4401; Mon–Sat 11am–9.30pm; station: Tsukiji; ¥¥¥

An old-school sushi emporium, cavernous but packed. The portions are generous, and the location near Tsukiji Fish Market ensures they are fresh.

Icho
Hotel Nikko Tokyo, 1-9-1 Daiba, Minato-ku; tel: 5500 5500; daily 11.30am–2.30pm and 5.30–9.30pm; station: Daiba; ¥¥¥¥

Teppanyaki – meat, fish and vegetables prepared on the griddle in front of you – in a romantic setting that overlooks the Rainbow Bridge.

Above from far left: bamboo baskets of steamed root vegetables; *unagi* (eel) being grilled.

NIGHTLIFE

The last-but-certainly-not-least hours in Tokyo's 24-hour day are a time when busy urbanites unwind at the city's fathomless horizon of 'live house' music venues, dance clubs and DJ bars. The only challenge is deciding when and where to go. Live-music venues usually start and end early; DJ bars and dance clubs pick up from there until mid-morning at weekends. Tokyo nightlife tends to be a safe and friendly experience; still, the usual caution is advisable. Due to police vigilance over drugs and under-age drinking, many clubs enforce a 20-and-over policy; photo ID is a must.

Bars

A971 Garden < > House
Tokyo Midtown, 9-7-3 Akasaka, Minato-ku; tel: 5413 7340; www.a971.com/tokyo; Mon–Thur 10am–2am, Fri–Sat 10am–5am, Sun 10am–midnight; station: Roppongi
Stylish café-bar at the front of the Midtown complex, where the wide choice of reasonably priced drinks and food and free internet always attract a crowd.

Cuzn
1-41-8 Asakusa, Taitÿ-ku; tel: 3842 3223; www.cuzn.jp; daily 11am–5pm; station: Asakusa Tsukuba Express or Tawaramachi
This foreigner-friendly bar is a relaxed spot with good food, free internet access and sport playing on a big-screen TV.

Fiesta International Karaoke Bar
3F Crest Roppongi-1, 7-9-3 Roppongi, Minato-ku; tel: 5410 3008; www.fiesta-roppongi.com; Mon–Sat 7pm–5am; station: Roppongi
A legendary English-language karaoke bar with over 10,000 international hits and 70,000 Japanese songs catering to an international crowd. There's a good sound system and two 50-inch TVs.

The Footnik
1F Asahi Building, 1-11-2 Ebisu, Shibuya-ku; tel: 5795 0144; www.footnik.net; Mon–Fri 11.30–1am, Sat, Sun and hols 3pm–1am; station: Ebisu
This British football pub draws expats and Japanese football fans alike with big-screen TVs. There's another branch in Osaki (1F ThinkPark, 2-1-1 Osaki, Shinagawa-ku; tel: 5759 1044).

Heartland
1F Roppongi Hills West Walk, 6-10-1 Roppongi, Minato-ku; tel: 5772 7600; www.heartland.jp; daily 11am–5am; station: Roppongi
A stylish standing-room-only DJ bar in the northwest corner of Roppongi Hills – it's a lively pick-up joint but not sleazy.

New York Bar
52F Park Hyatt Hotel, 3-7-1-2 Nishi Shinjuku, Shinjuku-ku; tel: 5323 3458; http://tokyo.park.hyatt.com; daily 5pm–midnight, Thur–Sat until 1am; station: Tochomae

Located on the upper floors of the luxurious Park Hyatt Hotel, this spot is popular because of its night views over Tokyo. The drinks list is impressive and the service impeccable. There's a ¥2,000 cover charge from 8pm (7pm on Sun).

Old Imperial Bar
Imperial Hotel, 1-1-1 Uchisaiwai-cho, Hibiya, Chiyoda-ku; tel: 3504 1111; www.imperialhotel.co.jp; daily 11.30am–midnight; station: Hibiya

The hotel's legendary bar is the only part of it that preserves the original Frank Lloyd Wright Art Deco design from the 1920s. Order their original Mount Fuji cocktail. *See also p.35.*

The Pink Cow
B1F Villa Moderna, 1-3-18 Shibuya, Shibuya-ku; tel: 3406 5597; www.thepinkcow.com; Tue–Sun 5pm until late; station: Shibuya

Loved by the art, fashion and media crowd, this café-bar offers a good range of wine, beers and cocktails as well as food. Events include poetry readings, jazz concerts, book launches and art exhibitions.

Sekirei
Meiji Kinenkan, 2-2-23 Moto-Akasaka, Minato-ku; tel: 3746 7723; www.meijikinenkan.gr.jp; July–end Aug Mon–Sat 4.30–10.30pm, Sun 5.30–10.30pm; station: Shinanomachi

At this elegant summer-only bar, inside the grand Meiji Kinenkan wedding and party hall, look out on a garden where classical Japanese dance is performed nightly.

T.Y. Harbor Brewery
2-1-3 Higashi-Shinagawa, Shingawa-ku; tel: 5479 4555; www.tyharbor brewing.co.jp; daily 11.30am–2pm and 5.30–10pm; stations: Tennozu Isle and Shinagawa; ¥¥

A canalside venue serving microbrewed ales and high-quality American bar food. English menu.

Gay Bars

Advocates Café
1F 7th Tenka Building, 2-18-1 Shinjuku, Shinjuku-ku; tel: 3358 3988; advocates-cafe.com; Wed–Sun 6pm–4am; station: Shinjuku-Sanchome

A well-known and friendly spot among the expat and local gay crowd, and a good place to begin your Shinjuku Ni-chome wanderings.

Arty Farty
2-11-7 Shinjuku, Shinjuku-ku; tel: 5362 9720; www.arty-farty.net; Mon 7pm–midnight, Tue–Fri 7pm–5am, Sat–Sun 5pm–5am; station: Shinjuku-Sanchome

Gay dance bar with a mostly male clientele, although an exception is made on Sundays when women accompanied by gay male friends are allowed in.

Above from far left: young urbanites hanging out; the Pink Cow café-bar in Shibuya.

Tickets
Concert tickets can be purchased at box offices, ticket agency Pia (found in major department stores) and convenience store Lawson. If your Japanese is up to snuff, Pia (http://t.pia.jp) and e+ (http://eplus.jp) both offer online ticketing. English-language listings are available in the *Metropolis* (http://metropolis.co.jp) and the daily newspapers, as well as Tokyo Gig Guide (www.tokyogigguide.com) and iFlyer (www.iflyer.jp/tokyo).

The Lounge Arty Farty

Shinjuku's Gay Scene

Most of Shinjuku Ni-chome's 300 or more hole-in-the-wall gay clubs and bars generally do not welcome casual visitors or foreigners who do not speak Japanese. The listed venues are both welcoming to all comers and relatively easy to find.

GB

B1F, Business Shinjuku Plaza Building, 2-12-3 Shinjuku, Shinjuku-ku; tel: 3352 8972; www.techtrans-japan.com/GB/index.htm; daily 8pm–2am, Fri–Sat until 3am; station: Shinjuku-Sanchome

A men-only venue that is one of the favourite spots in Tokyo for meetings between foreigners and locals.

Live Jazz

Billboard Live

4F Tokyo Midtown, 9-7-4 Akasaka, Minato-ku; tel: 3405 1133; www.billboard-live.com; shows Mon–Fri 7 and 9.30pm, Sat–Sun and hols 6 and 9pm; station: Roppongi

Licensed by the American music industry trade magazine *Billboard*, this glistening international jazz and pop supper club is a centrepiece of Roppongi's Tokyo Midtown development.

Blue Note Tokyo

6-3-16 Minami-Aoyama, Minato-ku; tel: 5485 0088; www.bluenote.co.jp; station: Omotesando

Top international acts appear in this sophisticated venue. The ambience is much like that of the original venue in the US.

Pit Inn

B1F Accord Building, 2-12-4 Shinjuku, Shinjuku-ku; tel: 3354 2024; www.pit-inn.com; station: Shinjuku-Sanchome

For over 40 years, Pit Inn has been a temple of jazz for the Tokyo faithful, featuring avant-garde innovators like Yoshihide Otomo and the occasional overseas act. Evening entry is ¥3,000 including one drink.

Live Popular Music

Club Asia

1-8 Maruyama-cho, Shibuya-ku; tel: 5458 5963; www.clubasia.co.jp; station: Shibuya

The dance floors and bars on different levels are an interesting design feature, although the music can get warped in the process. Typical of Tokyo's multi-use spaces, Club Asia might host a punk band in the evening, followed by a night of club jazz, trance or dancehall.

Club Quattro

5F Parco Quattro, 32-13 Udagawacho, Shibuya-ku; tel: 3477 8750; www.club-quattro.com; Shibuya

International rock and world music bands as well as local groups play at this intimate venue, which is one of Tokyo's most storeyed stages.

Crocodile

B1, 6-18-8 Jingumae, Shibuya-ku; tel: 3499 5205; www.music.co.jp/~croco; shows 8pm; station: Shibuya

One of the oldest live-music venues in Tokyo, Crocodile has expanded its repertoire over the years to include not just rock, but whatever happens to be hip, including rap bands, Latin combos and jazz. Also hosts English shows by the Tokyo Comedy Store (www.tokyocomedy.com).

Liquid Room
3-16-6 Higashi, Shibuya-ku; tel: 5464 0800; www.liquidroom.net; station: Ebisu

A roomy basement venue with a lounge bar and an excellent line-up of rock concerts and DJs. Upstairs is a Tower Records café, which often hosts late-night house parties.

SuperDeluxe
B1F, 3-1-25 Nishi Azabu, Minato-ku; tel: 5412 0515; www.super-deluxe.com; Mon–Sat 6pm–late; station: Roppongi

This spacious basement, a self-proclaimed 'place of experimentation', assumes a different character depending on the event. A night of cutting-edge electronica may be followed by a contemporary dance performance or avant-garde fashion show. Crowds vary, but the atmosphere is always friendly. Check out their Pecha Kucha nights (www.pecha-kucha.org), when Tokyo's creative get to show and tell.

Dance Clubs

Ageha
2-2-10 Shin-Kiba, Koto-ku; tel: 5534 1515; www.ageha.com; Fri–Sat 11pm–late; station: Shin-Kiba

Tokyo's biggest dance club, with three separate dance rooms and a poolside bar. Hundreds of clubbers bus in from Shibuya for massive hip-hop, house, techno and trance parties.

Air
2-11 Sarugaku, Shibuya-ku; tel: 5784 3386; www.air-tokyo.com; Mon–Sat 10pm–late; station: Shibuya

Between Shibuya and trendy Daikan-yama, Air is a comfortable mid-sized dance club that competes with Tokyo's leading venues for young, ultra-hip clubbers looking to dance to house, electro, drum 'n' bass and hip-hop. There's a café upstairs for chilling out.

Warehouse 702
B1F Fukao Building, 1-4-5 Azabu-juban, Minato-ku; tel: 6230 0343; www.warehouse702.com; Mon–Sat from 10 or 11pm; station: Azabu-juban

One of Tokyo's larger clubs, this long, narrow underground space with a stage at one end and a bar at the other promises radical sounds and fashions.

Womb
2-16 Maruyama-cho, Shibuya-ku; tel: 5459 0039; www.womb.co.jp; Fri–Sat 10pm–late, Sun 4–10pm; station: Shibuya

This cavernous four-floor club is one of the serious dance-culture venues in Tokyo. What it lacks in atmosphere it makes up for with excellent music and a gargantuan sound system.

Above from far left: ordering a drink in a Roppongi bar; gay dance bar; cocktail at the Park Hyatt's New York Grill; live music at SuperDeluxe.

CREDITS

Insight Step by Step Tokyo
Written/updated by: Stephen Mansfield and Simon Richmond
Series Editor: Clare Peel
Commissioning Editor: Alex Knights
Cartography Editors: Zoë Goodwin, James Macdonald and Neal Jordan-Caws
Map Production: Stephen Ramsay
Picture Manager: Steven Lawrence
Art Editor: Ian Spick
Deputy Art Editor: Richard Cooke
Production: Patrick Tan
Photography: All by Ming Tang Evans/APA and Richard Nowitz/APA, except APA 24; TWPhoto/Corbis 114–5; Getty 29TR, 40–1, 47, 76, 77; Hiromy 56; iStockphoto 13TL, 16TL, 30, 30–1, 38–9, 55, 62, 73, 78T, 84T, 86, 91, 92, 95T; Jack Vs Japan 52T; Japanese National Tourist Organisation 15T, 31TR, 58–9, 80, 82–3, 84–5, 85, 87, 88, 90, 92–3, 93, 94, 95B, 98–9, 114, 115; Leonardo 97–8, 97/5, 109, 112, 113; Stephen Mansfield/APA 57, 58; Mary Evans 25; Darren Ruane/onasia.com 81; Mark Henley/Panos Pictures 50–1; Sinopix/Rex Features 49; Scala Archives 34–5; Tips Images 43; Udono 70
Front cover: main image: Corbis; bottom left and right: APA.
Inside back cover: Tokyo Subway Route Map © Bureau of Transportation Tokyo Metropolitan Government

Acknowledgements: Simon – Many thanks to Tonny for joining me for Christmas and Toshiko Kiyama and Takekawa-san for their assistance.

Printed by: CTPS-China

© 2009 APA Publications GmbH & Co. Verlag KG (Singapore branch)
All rights reserved

First Edition 2009, Reprinted 2011
No part of this book may be reproduced, stored in a retrieval system or transmitted in any form or by any means (electronic, mechanical, photocopying, recording or otherwise), without prior written permission of APA Publications. Brief text quotations with use of photographs are exempted for book review purposes only. Information has been obtained from sources believed to be reliable, but its accuracy and completeness, and the opinions based thereon, are not guaranteed.

Although Insight Guides and the authors of this book have taken all reasonable care in preparing it, we make no warranty about the accuracy or completeness of its content, and, to the maximum extent permitted, disclaim all liability arising from its use.

CONTACTING THE EDITORS

We would appreciate it if readers would alert us to errors or outdated information by writing to us at insight@apaguide.co.uk or APA Publications, PO Box 7910, London SE1 1WE, UK.

www.insightguides.com

DISTRIBUTION

Worldwide
APA Publications GmbH & Co. Verlag KG (Singapore branch)
7030 Ang Mo Kio Ave 5
08-65 Northstar @ AMK, Singapore 569880
Email: apasin@singnet.com.sg

UK and Ireland
GeoCenter International Ltd
Meridian House, Churchill Way West
Basingstoke, Hampshire RG21 6YR
Email: sales@geocenter.co.uk

US
Ingram Publisher Services
One Ingram Blvd, PO Box 3006
La Vergne, TN 37086-1986
Email: customer.service@ingrampublisherservices.com

Australia
Universal Publishers
PO Box 307
St. Leonards NSW 1590
Email: sales@universalpublishers.com.au

New Zealand
Hema Maps New Zealand Ltd (HNZ)
Unit 2
10 Cryers Road
East Tamaki
Auckland 2013
Email: sales.hema@clear.net.nz

INDEX

109 Building **48–9**
21_21 Design Sight **38**

A

accommodation **108–113**
Akasaka **36, 41**
Akasaka Biz Tower **41**
Akihabara **23**
Ameya Yokocho **61**
AMLUX **64**
Ancient Orient Museum **64**
anime (Japanese animation) **23**
Aoyama **42–3**
Aoyama Theatre **23**
Ark Hills **40–1**
Art Triangle Roppongi project **36**
Asakusa **10, 11, 19, 66–9**
Asakura Choso Museum **57**
Asakusa Hanayashiki amusement park **68**
Asakusa-jinja **67–8**
Audi Forum **45**
Azabu Die Pratze (*butoh* venue) **23**

B

Benten-do, Ueno Park **61**
Book 1st **53**
Bridgestone Museum of Art **34**
Bunkamura **22, 48**

C

Centre Gai (street) **48**
cherry blossom **12, 17, 28, 54, 60**
children **98**
Chinzan-so (garden) **65**
Chuo-dori **32, 35, 50**
climate **12**
Comme des Garçons **42**
Crafts Gallery (Kogeikan) **30**
cruise (Sumida River) **69**

D

Daibutsu (Great Buddha) **87**
Daien-ji **58**
dance **22–3**
Decks Tokyo Beach **79**
Design Festa **44**
Dogenzaka **48**
Dream Island **11**
drink **17**
Drum Museum **69**

E

Ebisu **46, 49**
Edo **10–11, 15, 52, 72–3, 80**
Edo-Tokyo Museum **72–3**
Eitai-bashi (bridge) **72**
embassies **99–100**
Enoshima **87**
entertainment **21–3**
etiquette **12, 16, 100**

F

festivals **12, 28, 40, 66, 69, 72, 82**
food **14–7, 114–19**
Fuji TV Building **79**
Fukagawa **70–2**
Fukagawa Edo Museum **70**
Fukagawa Fudo-do **72**

G

Gallery Ma **38**
Ghibli Museum **23**
Ginza **19, 32, 35, 69**
Ginza 4-chome **35**
Gokoku-ji **65**
Golden Gai **55**
Grand Hyatt Hotel **38, 109**
Great Kanto Earthquake **13, 30, 52, 56, 73**

H

Hachiko statue **47**
Hakone **13, 88–91**
 Hakone Art Museum **90**
 Hakone Open-Air Museum **89–90**
 Hakone-Yumoto **88**
 Lake Ashino **91**
 Owakudani **90**
Hama Rikyu Garden **69**
Hanazono-jinja **54–5**
Harajuku **10, 19, 42, 44–5**
Hase **86–7**
Hibiya Park **31**
Hie-jinja **41**
Hinokicho Park **37**
history **24–5**

I

Idemitsu Museum of Art **32–3**
Ikebukuro **62–5**
Imperial Hotel **22, 35, 108**
Imperial Music Hall **31**
Imperial Palace **10, 28–31**
Imperial Palace East Garden **30–1**
Imperial Palace Plaza **30–1**
Isetan department store **14, 18, 54**
Isetatsu (shop) **58**

J

Japan Folk Crafts Museum **46–7**
Japan Traditional Crafts Centre **62**
Jingu Naien (garden) **45**
Jingu Stadium **20**
Jiyu Gakuen Myonichikan **63**
Jomyo-in **59**

K

kabuki 21–2, 35
Kabukicho 50, 55
Kabuki-za theatre 22, 35, 55
Kamakura 13, 42, 84–6
 Engaku-ji 84
 Kanagawa Prefectural Museum of Modern Art 86
 Kencho-ji 85
 Tokei-ji 84–5
 Tsurugaoka Hachiman-gu 86
Kantei (Prime Minister's residence) 41
Kappabashi 69
Kawagoe 13, 80–3
 Gohyaku Rakan 83
 Honmaru Goten 82
 Kawagoe Festival Hall 82
 Kita-in 83
 Kumano-jinja 80
 Kurazukuri Shiryokan 81
 Osawa Jutaku (merchant house) 82
 Toki-no-Kane belltower 81
 Yamazaki Museum of Art 81
K-Ballet Company 22
Kiddyland 44
Kinokuniya bookshop 53–4
Kitanomaru Park 29–30
Kiyomizu Kannon-do 60–1
Kiyosu-bashi (bridge) 71–2
Kiyosumi Garden 71
Koma Theatre 55
Kotoku-in 86–7
Kyu-Yasuda Garden 73

L

La Collezione 42
Lake Chuzenji 94
Living Design Centre Ozae 51
Lloyd Wright, Frank 35, 63

M

Maman sculpture 38
manga (Japanese comics) 23
markets 55, 61, 72, 83
martial arts 20, 72
Marunouchi 19, 32–4
Meiji-jingu 10, 45
Mejirodai 65
Midtown Tower, Roppongi 36–7, 40
Miraikan *see* National Museum of Emerging Science and Innovation
Mitsubishi Ichigokan Museum 33–4
Mitsukoshi department store 14, 18, 35, 54
Miyake, Issey 37, 42
Miyamoto Unosuke Shoten (shop) 68–9
Miyazaki, Hayao 23
Mode Gakuen Cocoon Tower 52–3
money 102
Mori Art Museum 36, 39
Mori Tower 38–40
Mount Fuji 13, 50, 90
Musée Tomo 40
Museum of Maritime Science 79
music 23
Myth of Tomorrow (painting) 46–7

N

Naka-dori 32
Namco Namjatown (theme park) 64
Naritasan Betsu-in 83
National Art Centre 36, 38
National Diet Building 41
National Museum of Emerging Science and Innovation 78
National Museum of Modern Art 30
National Museum of Western Art 59–60
National Noh Theatre 22
National Stadium 21
National Sumo Stadium 20, 73
National Theatre 22
National Yoyogi Stadium 45
New National Theatre 22–3, 52
Nezu Museum of Art 42–3
nightlife 120–23
Nijubashi (Double Layer Bridge) 31
Nikko 12–3, 92–5
 Futarasan-jinja 95
 Meiji-no-Yakata 95
 Nikko Tosho-gu Museum of Art 95
 Taiyuin-byo 95
 Tosho-gu 92–4
Nippon Budokan 20, 30
Nogi-jinja 38
NTT Intercommunication Centre 52

O

Odaiba 11, 72, 78–9
Oedo Antiques Market 33
Oedo Onsen Monogatari (hot-spring) 78
Old Imperial Bar 35
Olympic Games 45, 65
Omotesando Hills 18, 44
opening hours 18, 101
Orchard Hall 22, 48
Oriental Bazaar 19, 44
Ota Memorial Museum of Art 45
Otaku culture 23
Owakudani 90

P

Palette Town 78
Park Hyatt Hotel 51, 111
Peninsula Tokyo 32, 108
population 10–11
Prada 42

R

Rainbow Bridge 79
Reigan-ji 71

restaurants **114–19**
Rikkyo University **62–3**
Roppongi **36–41**
Roppongi Crossing **36**
Roppongi Hills **18**, **36**, **38–9**, **64**
Ryogoku **11**, **72–3**

S

Saigo Takamori statue **60–1**
St Mary's Cathedral **65**
Sakurada-mon **31**
SCAI The Bathhouse **58**
Seiji Togo Memorial Sompo Japan Museum of Art **53**
Senso-ji **67–8**
Session House **23**
Shakaden **40**
Shiba Park **40**
Shibuya **19**, **46–9**
Shimbashi Embujo theatre **22**, **35**
Shimokitazawa district **22**
Shinjuku **50–5**
Shinjuku Chuo Park **51**
Shinjuku National Garden **54**
Shinjuku Park Tower **51**
Shinkansen (bullet train) **35**, **106**
Shinobazu Pond **61**
Shiseido Gallery **35**
Shitamachi ('Low City') **11**, **56–61**, **66**
Shitamachi Museum **61**
Shomben Yokocho **53**
shopping **18–9**, **62**, **67–8**
Sky Deck, Mori Tower **39**
Sompo Japan Building **53**
Sony Building **35**
sports **20–1**
Studio Alta **53**
Sumida-gawa-ohashi (bridge) **72**
Sumitomo Building **52**
Sumiyoshi-jinja **77**
Sunshine City **64**
Suntory Hall **41**
Suntory Museum of Art **36**, **37**
Super Dry Hall **69**

T

Taiwan-kaku Pavilion **54**
Takashimaya department store **18**
Takashimaya Times Square **54**
Takeshita-dori **45**
Takurazuka Theatre **22**
Tayasu-mon **29**
Tenno-ji **57**
Tenyasu Honten (shop) **77**
Tepco Electric Energy Museum **47**
theatre **21–2**
Tobacco and Salt Museum **47**
Togo-jinja **44**
Tokyo Anime Centre **23**
Tokyo Big Sight **78**
Tokyo City View, Mori Tower **39**
Tokyo Dome **20**
Tokyo International Forum **19**, **33**
Tokyo Ireido complex **73**
Tokyo Magazine Centre **53**
Tokyo Metropolitan Art Museum **60**
Tokyo Metropolitan Art Space **62**
Tokyo Metropolitan Festival Hall **60**
Tokyo Metropolitan Government Office **40**, **50**
Tokyo Metropolitan Photography Museum **49**
Tokyo Midtown **36–8**, **64**
Tokyo National Museum **56**, **59**
Tokyo Opera City **22**, **52**
Tokyo Sky Tree **40**
Tokyo Station **34**
Tokyo Tower **23**, **39–40**
Tokyo Wonder Site **48**
Tokyu Hands **48**, **54**, **64**
Tomioka Hachiman-gu **72**
Toraya (shop) **17**
tourist information centres **50–1**, **66**, **80**, **84**, **89**, **93**, **104**
tours **13**, **31**, **50–1**, **59**, **66**
tramway **65**
transport **11**, **65**, **69**, **104–7**
Tsukiji Fish Market **15**, **69**, **74–5**, **77**
Tsukiji Hongan-ji **75**
Tsukudajima **76–7**

U

Ueno **18–9**
Ueno Park **56**, **59–61**
Ueno Zoo **60**
Urban Dock LaLaport Toyosu **77**

V

Venus Fort mall **18**, **78**
visas **107**

W

Wadakura Fountain Park **31**
Wako department store **35**
waterbuses **69**, **72**

Y

Yanaka **56–7**
Yanaka Cemetery **56–7**
Yanaka Ginza **57**
Yasakuni-jinja **10**, **20**, **28–9**
Yebisu Beer Museum **49**
Yebisu Garden Place **49**
Yokoami Park **73**
Yokozuna Monument **72**
Yoshidaya Sake-ten (museum) **58–9**
Yoyogi Park **45**
Yushukan (museum) **29**

Z

Zenshi (galleries) **71**
Zojo-ji **40**
Zoshigaya Cemetery **65**

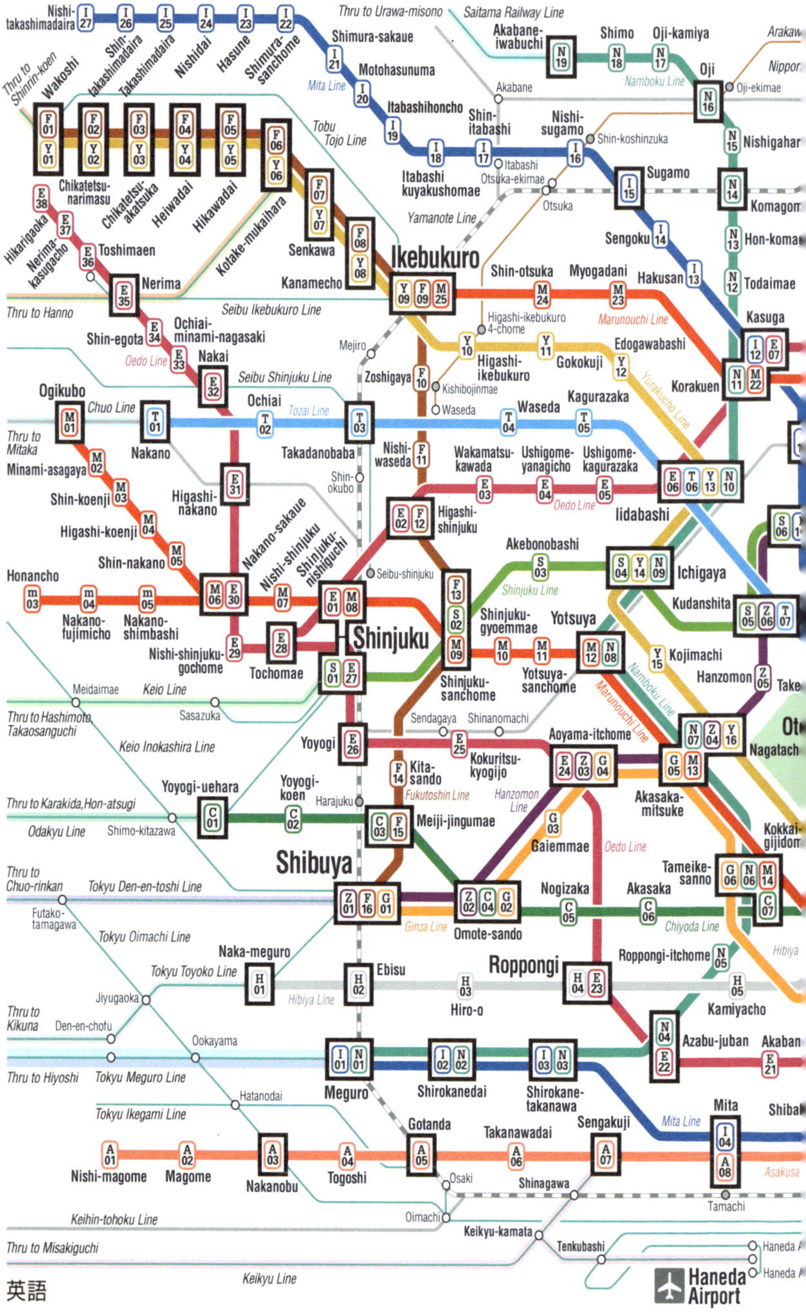
Nishi-takashimadaira
Shin-takashimadaira
Takashimadaira
Nishidai
Hasune
Shimura-sanchome
Shimura-sakaue
Motohasunuma
Itabashihoncho
Shin-itabashi
Nishi-sugamo
Itabashi kuyakushomae
Sugamo
Sengoku
Hakusan
Kasuga
Thru to Shinrin-koen
Wakoshi
Chikatetsu-narimasu
Chikatetsu-akatsuka
Heiwadai
Hikawadai
Kotake-mukaihara
Senkawa
Kanamecho
Ikebukuro
Hikarigaoka
Nerima-kasugacho
Toshimaen
Nerima
Thru to Hanno
Seibu Ikebukuro Line
Shin-egota
Ochiai-minami-nagasaki
Oedo Line
Nakai
Seibu Shinjuku Line
Thru to Urawa-misono
Saitama Railway Line
Akabane-iwabuchi
Shimo
Oji-kamiya
Oji
Oji-ekimae
Arakaw
Nippor
Namboku Line
Akabane
Mita Line
Tobu Tojo Line
Shin-koshinzuka
Nishigahar
Komagom
Hon-koma
Todaimae
Itabashi
Otsuka-ekimae
Otsuka
Yamanote Line
Shin-otsuka
Myogadani
Marunouchi Line
Higashi-ikebukuro 4-chome
Mejiro
Zoshigaya
Higashi-ikebukuro
Gokokuji
Edogawabashi
Yurakucho Line
Korakuen
Kishibojinmae
Waseda
Ogikubo
Chuo Line
Thru to Mitaka
Nakano
Ochiai
Tozai Line
Takadanobaba
Kagurazaka
Minami-asagaya
Shin-koenji
Higashi-koenji
Shin-nakano
Higashi-nakano
Nishi-waseda
Shin-okubo
Wakamatsu-kawada
Ushigome-yanagicho
Ushigome-kagurazaka
Iidabashi
Higashi-shinjuku
Akebonobashi
Shinjuku Line
Ichigaya
Kudanshita
Honancho
Nakano-fujimicho
Nakano-shimbashi
Nakano-sakaue
Nishi-shinjuku
Shinjuku-nishiguchi
Seibu-shinjuku
Shinjuku
Shinjuku-gyoemmae
Yotsuya
Kojimachi
Hanzomon
Take
Nishi-shinjuku-gochome
Tochomae
Shinjuku-sanchome
Yotsuya-sanchome
Meidaimae
Keio Line
Sasazuka
Thru to Hashimoto, Takaosanguchi
Keio Inokashira Line
Yoyogi
Sendagaya
Shinanomachi
Aoyama-itchome
Nagatach
Kokuritsu-kyogijo
Kita-sando
Yoyogi-uehara
Yoyogi-koen
Harajuku
Fukutoshin Line
Hanzomon Line
Akasaka-mitsuke
Thru to Karakida, Hon-atsugi
Odakyu Line
Shimo-kitazawa
Meiji-jingumae
Gaiemmae
Oedo Line
Kokkai-gijidom
Shibuya
Thru to Chuo-rinkan
Tokyu Den-en-toshi Line
Futako-tamagawa
Tokyu Oimachi Line
Nogizaka
Akasaka
Tameike-sanno
Ginza Line
Omote-sando
Chiyoda Line
Naka-meguro
Tokyu Toyoko Line
Ebisu
Roppongi
Roppongi-itchome
Hibiya
Hibiya Line
Hiro-o
Kamiyacho
Jiyugaoka
Thru to Kikuna
Den-en-chofu
Ookayama
Azabu-juban
Akaban
Thru to Hiyoshi
Tokyu Meguro Line
Meguro
Shirokanedai
Shirokane-takanawa
Hatanodai
Tokyu Ikegami Line
Gotanda
Takanawadai
Sengakuji
Mita Line
Mita
Shiba
Nishi-magome
Magome
Nakanobu
Togoshi
Osaki
Shinagawa
Asakusa
Tamachi
Keihin-tohoku Line
Oimachi
Keikyu-kamata
Thru to Misakiguchi
Tenkubashi
Haneda
Keikyu Line
Haneda Airport

英語